Y0-BYK-620

Rural Society in Japan

from

The Japan Foundation

Rural Society in Japan

Tadashi Fukutake

translated by
The Staff of *The Japan Interpreter*

UNIVERSITY OF TOKYO PRESS

Translation supported by a grant from the Ministry of Education, Science and Culture, and publication supported by a grant from The Japan Foundation.

Translated from the Japanese original
NIHON NO NŌSON, 2nd ed. (University of Tokyo Press, 1978)

English translation
© 1980 UNIVERSITY OF TOKYO PRESS
UTP Number 3036-57097-5149
ISBN 0-86008-266-0

Printed in Japan

Contents

Tables

Preface

In 1964 I completed the work that turned out to be the direct forebear of this one. Entitled *Nippon nōson shakairon*, it was translated into English by Professor Ronald P. Dore and published in 1967 by the Oxford University Press under the title *Japanese Rural Society*. A paperback edition was put out by Cornell University Press in 1972.

If it has been of any value, *Japanese Rural Society* may provide readers a better understanding of village life in Japan, past and present. Many elements in village life are enduring, but much has changed in the intervening years. That work deals with the Japanese village as it was until around 1960, before the period of rapid economic growth virtually restructured the Japanese economy and many areas of society as well. The original Japanese work was thoroughly revised to take account of the changes and published as *Nippon no nōson* in 1971. After further revision and updating of information, the second edition of *Nippon no nōson* came out in 1978. The present volume, *Rural Society in Japan*, is a translation of the 1978 edition. It is intended to keep readers abreast of the changes that have taken place in our rural areas since the work for *Japanese Rural Society* was completed sixteen years ago.

Japan's phenomenal economic growth in the past two decades

has had as great an impact on rural society as on agriculture. Many new developments seem to be positive; farm household income, for example, has increased tremendously through non-farming work. But agriculture itself is beset with increasingly serious difficulties, and so far there are no visible solutions. The situation is indeed severe when people can remark, "While farmers prosper, their farms are ruined." Rural society, too, has changed drastically, and not necessarily for the better. At the same time political attitudes and behavior of farmers have not changed enough to generate the kind of strength needed in a democratic society to promote and guard their own interests in balance with the interests of others.

If this book imparts nothing else, I hope that it will convey a realistic picture of the consequences of rapid economic growth. Rapid growth can bring as much harm as gain to both agriculture and the rural community. Thus I have tried to describe the magnitude of problems that confront Japanese agriculture and rural society, problems that have been pushed into the shadow while attention remains focused on the so-called miracle of our economic growth. Finally, I hope *Rural Society in Japan* will serve the members of the International Rural Sociological Association as a useful reference in their work in comparative rural sociology.

I would like to express sincere thanks to the staff of *The Japan Interpreter* for translating this book. While this translation is entirely new, the translators have tried to retain the English terminology used in Professor Dore's translation for the sake of continuity between the two works. Special thanks also go to the University of Tokyo Press for its careful editorial and production work.

Rural Society in Japan

Chapter One

Change in Rural Society

Development of Postwar Agriculture

Prewar Landholding System

From the beginning of the Meiji era (1868–1912) to World War II, agriculture was the task to which 5.5 million households, or 13.7 million individuals, devoted almost all their working lives. As of 1870, farmers made up about 80 percent of the labor force, but as the population grew, the proportion of farmers decreased, even though their absolute numbers remained constant.

Agriculture provided the springboard for Japan's industrialization and economic development, but prewar industry never absorbed enough of the farming population to reduce the real number of farming households. Industry merely held down significant increases in farm families by absorbing all sons below the eldest.

Rapid economic development could not, in any case, prevent the steady growth of a potential population surplus in rural society. An agricultural people since ancient times, Japanese cultivated every square foot of arable land, but the area tilled by the average farming family rarely came to more than a hectare. The average landlord did not have to employ the methods of capitalism in land management, which would entail hiring necessary farm labor, because he could freely use the labor already built into the large farm families—in effect, surplus labor. He continued to rent out small plots of land to family units, and that served to perpetuate the basic small-scale, family-enterprise nature of Japanese agriculture throughout the seven centuries of the medieval, early modern, and modern periods.

As Table 1 shows, the number of farmers who operated 5 or more hectares was negligible during the early years of this century, and about 70 percent operated farms of 1 hectare or less. Families with 1 to 2 hectares tended to increase slightly, while those with either 0.5 or less or 3 to 5 hectares declined. Farm size seemed to reach a standard about midway between those figures, but other than that there was no major change until after the postwar land reform. When the area of land under cultivation is a mere hectare or less it is almost impossible to live on what the land produces; particularly when the area drops to 0.5 hectare or less. No family working such a small plot could even hope to subsist on farming. Such families were forced to do some profitable outside work in addition to agriculture. Even the inaccurate statistics available from before the war show that 30 percent of farm families engaged in some sort of non-farm, cash-producing work. The 1938 Comprehensive Farm Survey reported that 31 percent of farm families derived some of their income from non-agricultural occupations and 24 percent actually acquired more income from other occupations than from farming. In 1941 these figures had become 37 percent and 21 percent respectively, so that by the end of the prewar period, well over half of all farm families were working at some occupation in addition to farming.

Table 1   Farm Households by Size of Operated Holding (percent)

Year	Size of Holding (ha)					
	≤0.5	≤1.0	≤2.0	≤3.0	≤5.0	≥5.0
1910	37.6	33.0	19.3	5.9	2.9	1.3
1920	35.3	33.3	20.7	6.1	2.8	1.6
1930	34.3	34.3	22.1	5.7	2.3	1.3
1940	33.3	32.8	24.5	5.7	2.2	1.4

Even if the land worked by a farm family does not increase in area, if productivity rises, the standard of living should also rise. Between the 1880s and about 1915, yields for rice, Japan's staple crop, increased by half, and by the beginning of the Shōwa era

(1926–) they had increased by another 20 percent. But increases in productivity were offset by relative declines in agricultural prices and a rising standard of living. Given no chance to find work in industry, the farmer continued to produce as long as he could scrape a meager existence out of the land. To make things worse, prices of farm products remained low. The economy of self-sufficiency that the farmer once knew had collapsed, leaving him to struggle in a commodity economy. As the standard of living kept on climbing, small increments in income became next to useless in the farmer's effort to rise out of poverty. Without significantly higher income, he was unable to accumulate enough capital to allow him to mechanize farm operations and raise productivity. He was forced to concentrate on raising productivity per unit by pouring in more labor instead. Any increases were achieved chiefly through the introduction of improved crop strains and ever more fertilizer. Some farm operations were mechanized by the late 1920s, usually threshing by machine. The remaining processes, with the exception of those that could be performed by horse- or ox-powered implements, remained bound to manual methods of production, and agriculture was unable to move out of that stage.

The old adage about farm life, "Leave in the morning, the stars still shining, return at night, walking on moonlight shadows" may overstate the situation somewhat, but it conveys how hard the prewar farmer had to work. Even then, after working long hours from before dawn until after dusk, economic well-being was still a long way off.

In addition to the disadvantage of small plots of land, almost half were rented from landlords at very high rates. At the beginning of the Meiji era, according to estimates, more than one-fourth of all farmland was cultivated by tenants. In 1872, when a land tax reform was enacted, 29 percent of land under cultivation was tenant land, and that proportion rapidly rose during the ensuing years of change in the economy. Fifteen years later tenant land made up 40 percent of the total, and by 1930 it reached a new peak of 47 percent. About 40 percent of farmers worked tenant land and owned their own plots as well, while close to 30 percent were pure tenant farmers with no land of their own (see Table 2).

Table 2   Farm Households by Ownership Status (percent)

Year	Owner-farmers	Part-owners / Part-tenants	Tenants
1910	32.8	39.5	27.8
1920	30.7	40.9	28.4
1930	30.6	42.6	26.8
1940	30.5	42.4	27.1

Looking at the figures we can identify a tendency in the Meiji era for the number of tenant farmers with no land of their own to rise, while the number of tenant-owners rose during and after the Taishō era (1912–26). From the beginning of Meiji onward, however, owner-farmers were not generally more than one-third the total number of farmers. Landlord-tenant relationships were a very important element in the prewar structure of Japanese agriculture. They were of course affected by the very high rents demanded by landlords, and the huge numbers of farmers involved, but most crucial in the landlord-tenant relationship was the tenuous nature of rights the tenant held regarding the land he worked, and the incontestable priority of ownership rights held by the landowner. The landlord was truly sovereign in his realm; he made up the ruling class in agricultural society. Landlord control of the village naturally changed character with time. Even though they look similar, there is a difference between the Meiji landlord, who worked to establish farm associations and helped improve agricultural technology, and the Taishō-Shōwa landlord, who was central in the creation of agricultural cooperatives and in the restructuring and strengthening of the village organization after the peasant strife of the post–World War I years.

The Meiji landlord eventually withdrew from active participation in farming and retreated into a parasitic existence, relinquishing direct control of the village while continuing to benefit from it. The Taishō-Shōwa landlord emerged to fill in the vacuum created by absentee landlords, becoming both active cultivator and the chief force in village control. Shifting patterns in village leadership also modified the status of tenant and part-tenant farmers. But a completely new status for farmers was never possible through internal changes in the landlord system. They would have to wait until the system itself was destroyed, which would not happen until after World War II and the implementation of the land reform.

New Start for Tenants

The postwar land reform carried out under the Occupation opened up new possibilities for development in agriculture. Conflicts bred by the system of landownership and tenancy were suppressed during the war years to make way for total national mobilization, but they resurfaced soon afterward. Resolution favored the tenants this time, for one of the priorities in reconstructing Japan's bombed-out industry and rebuilding the economy was to check spiraling inflation, and that necessitated making provision for food by assuring a controlled, steady supply of low-priced rice. Mandatory rice production could be carried out only by lightening the burden on tenants of rent for land.

The government understood that reform of the landholding system was imperative, and in December 1945, only a few months after the surrender, a bill was presented to the Imperial Diet containing revisions of the Agricultural Land Adjustment Law. This bill is generally known as the first land reform, and it would have allowed landlords to keep up to five hectares of cultivated land, stipulating that 40 percent of tenant land would be taken from them within five years. SCAP, however, in its "Memorandum on Land Reform," instructed the Japanese government to go even further and "break the economic bondage which has enslaved Japanese farmers through centuries of feudal oppression." The original law was passed, but SCAP suspended its enforcement and ordered the government to carry out a more thorough land reform. This action laid the groundwork for the second reform begun the following year, 1946.

The new set of laws enabled the state to buy up all land owned by absentee landlords and all rented land exceeding one hectare owned by resident landlords. Land thus acquired by the state was resold at low prices to the tenants. The reform also prohibited payment of rents in kind; all rents were to be paid in cash, subject to controls that prevented exorbitant rates.

The land reform reduced the land farmed by tenants from the

pre-reform level of 53 percent of paddy and 40 percent of dry fields to well below 10 percent for both, turning long-established patterns upside down in little more than two years. As Table 3 shows, owner-farmers made up only slightly more than 30 percent of all farmers in 1946, but in four years their numbers doubled to 61.9 percent, and by 1975 they represented 84.1 percent of the total. The almost 30 percent of farmers who cultivated someone else's land exclusively in 1946 has now dropped to a negligible 1.1 percent.

Table 3   Farm Households by Ownership Status (percent)

Year	Owner-farmers	Part-owners / Part-tenants	Part-tenants / Part-owners	Tenants
1946	32.8	19.8	18.6	28.7
1950	61.9	25.8	6.6	5.1
1955	69.5	21.6	4.7	4.0
1960	75.2	18.0	3.6	2.9
1965	80.1	15.1	2.8	1.8
1970	79.4	16.0	2.8	1.6
1975	84.1	12.2	2.4	1.1

The 1946 land reform provided a direct stimulus for higher productivity, because once the farmer owned his land, he was motivated to produce more. In the past when tenure was insecure, the tenant farmer was reluctant to make any improvement in his land, knowing that the landlord might withdraw his tenancy rights at any time. In addition, the tenant did not have the kind of capital that improvements required. A further crucial factor that dampened motivation was that if the tenant increased his yield, there was a good chance the landlord would raise the rent. All told, the tenant farmer had little reason to try to raise agricultural productivity, but following the land reform, higher yields meant an immediate increase in income. The reform provided the incentive, and farmers plunged into learning new agricultural technology, setting up study groups all over the nation. The government also helped disseminate technological know-how through the newly established Agricultural Extension Service. Steady progress in the absorption and practical development of agricultural technology pushed up yields of the chief staple, rice, year after year. Before the land reform, a rice harvest of over

3,000 kgs. per hectare was considered a bumper crop, but by 1950 that had become average. Today the average crop is 4,500 kgs.; a yield of 4,700 kgs. or more is considered a bumper crop.

Production of wheat, once considered second in importance only to rice, has declined drastically, but in its place there has been a major increase in fruit production. Growth in livestock farming, particularly dairy, has also been remarkable. While farmers throughout the country had a total of only 20,000 head of dairy cows in 1930, by 1950 they had 200,000 and by 1960 they had 820,000. Although the number of cattle-raising families has declined sharply, the number of animals per family has increased and there are now 1,800,000 dairy cattle throughout the country.

Improved yields and diversification of farming moved forward hand in hand with mechanization. Before the land reform, farmers relied almost completely on animal and human power, and the number of agricultural machines used in Japan was negligible, but the use of small power cultivators has spread dramatically over the past several decades. The small hand-pushed gasoline-engine cultivator came into wider use around 1950, and by 1960 more than 500,000 were at work on farms. In 1978 the number had climbed to 3,300,000. A shift to larger, driver-seat tractors is now under way; 25,000 tractors of this type were in use in 1965, and more than 650,000 today. The combine was almost nonexistent in Japan during 1965, but 45,000 were in use by 1970 and 340,000 by 1975. Compared with 30,000 mechanized planters in 1970, there were 740,000 by 1975.

Widespread use of machines and higher productivity have brought far-reaching effects to Japan's agriculture, but its problems are far from being solved. On the contrary, the nation's farming is in a serious predicament. Postwar developments in agriculture, symbolized by the rapid dissemination of the power cultivator, have actually magnified the contradictions inherent in rural society. Mechanization based on the small power cultivator is possible in the small Japanese farm, but the necessary investment is still too high for most individual operators. More combines and large tractors, furthermore, have brought mechanization into a new phase of development with its own problems, leaving earlier ones unresolved. The dilemma today is how to continue without overinvesting in mechanization. This creates a crisis for farmers that so far has no answer. At the relatively simple stage of agriculture aided by the power cultivator, the Japanese farmer was using more energy per square meter of land than any other farmer in the world. As the nation moves on to a more advanced stage of mechanization, the waste will only multiply.

This situation developed in spite of the abolition of the landlord system and subsequent progress in agriculture, or perhaps because of it, for the simple reason that the Japanese farm is just too small. Even though the 1946–48 land reform was drastic, it could only go so far; it was a reform, not a revolution. Land reform transferred farm ownership into different hands, but it did nothing to consolidate holdings. If anything, they were further fragmented when farm families were swollen by returning soldiers after World War II. Table 4 shows a very slight rise and fall in

Table 4   Farm Households by Size of Operated Holding (percent)

Year	Size of Holding (ha)					
	≤0.5	≤1.0	≤2.0	≤3.0	≤5.0	≥5.0
1946	39.2	31.4	23.5	3.7	1.4	0.9
1950	40.8	31.9	21.7	3.4	1.3	0.8
1955	38.5	32.7	22.9	3.4	1.3	1.3
1960	38.3	31.7	23.6	3.8	1.5	1.0
1965	37.6	31.3	24.2	4.2	1.5	1.1
1970	37.9	30.2	24.1	4.8	1.7	1.3
1975	40.5	29.1	22.0	5.0	1.9	1.4

all landholding categories, but there have been no major changes since the end of the war. Farms remain about the same size and retain the same general distribution pattern as they did in the late forties. In 1955–60, 1 hectare was considered the minimum necessary area for viable full-time farming, and every five years this watershed has moved up 0.5 hectare to reach 2.5 hectares in 1970–75. Even then, no clear class differentiation in the farming population has taken place.

Farmers have been able to raise their yields, but small farm size places limits on what can be done. Farmers have increased their net income with bigger harvests, but costs of fertilizers, insecticides, herbicides, and germicides are constantly rising. Add to this the initial outlay and maintenance costs for machinery, and the farmer's financial burden becomes considerably heavy. Their standard of living has improved much more rapidly than before the war, but farming alone does not provide most farmers with the necessary margin to maintain or raise the standard, so they must seek outside income.

During the rapid growth years of the sixties, the gap between what farm income could provide and the outlay necessary to keep up with Japan's rising standard of living grew wider and wider. The struggle has been so discouraging that many farmers have given up and moved into other occupations, and many more are tempted. Agriculture has remained teetering in the balance for years, and farmers and observers alike warn that its future is precarious, but we still do not know which way it will go, and nothing substantial is being done to decide one way or the other.

Impact of Rapid Economic Growth

Around 1955 the economy shifted gears and moved from recovery to growth. Starting in 1960 the rate of growth began to rise vigorously and by 1968 Japan's GNP was second highest in the free world. The economy was third largest in the world after the United States and the Soviet Union. Rapidly rising growth rates were a direct result of advances in industry, particularly manufacturing, but even though the annual growth rate in GNP was 10 percent and higher during those years, farmers were hard pressed even to eke out a 3 percent growth rate in agriculture. In 1955 agriculture accounted for almost 20 percent of gross national income, but that rapidly declined to approximately 10 percent in 1960, and to less than 5 percent at present. Worse, the disparity in income between agriculture and other industries has continued to grow.

A decreasing rural population has also been draining the agricultural labor force year by year. Sixteen million people were working in farm occupations in 1950; by 1960 their number had dropped to the prewar level of 13.7 million, and by the end of 1967 to 10 million, or 20 percent of the entire national labor force. The precipitous plunge from 45.2 percent in 1950 to 30.1 percent in 1960 and then to 17.9 percent in 1970 was brought on by the simultaneous decline in numbers of people employed in farming and the rise in the total labor force, but even taking those factors into consideration it was still an impressive drop (see Table 5).

Table 5   Demographic Change and the Farming Population and Households (unit: ten thousand)

Year	Total Population (A)	Farm Population (B)	Total Households (C)	Farm Households (D)	Total Labor Force (E)	Farm Labor Force (F)	B/A	D/C	F/E
1950	8,320	3,767	1,642	618	3,563	1,610	45.3%	37.6%	45.2%
1955	8,928	3,635	1,738	604	3,926	1,489	40.7	34.8	37.9
1960	9,342	3,441	1,968	606	4,369	1,313	36.8	30.8	30.1
1965	9,828	3,008	2,309	567	4,761	1,086	30.6	24.6	22.8
1970	10,372	2,628	2,686	534	5,224	933	25.3	19.8	17.9
1975	11,193	2,319	3,139	495	5,314	672	20.7	15.8	12.6

Perhaps the major reason for the plummeting agricultural population has been the attraction of rapidly expanding industries which continue to absorb much of the farm labor force in their most productive years. What is a more immediate illustration than the present reluctance of those entering the job market to consider employment in agriculture? Twenty-five percent of all junior high, high school, and college graduates entered work in farming in 1950, but by 1960 that percentage had dropped to 10 and by 1965 to less than 5 percent. At the present time, only 10,000 people per year, or 1.3 percent of all graduates, are seeking jobs in farming. Twenty-five years ago the critical problem was to find employment for all of the farmers' sons besides the eldest, but only ten years later the major worry was to find someone to take over the farm.

The average age of the farm labor force has also risen steadily; in 1960 one quarter of those who carried the main responsibility for the farm were under 30, and this has dropped to 8 percent. At the opposite end of the spectrum, 50 percent were 40 or older, and that figure is now 75 percent. The aging problem stands out starkly when we find that in non-agricultural sectors more than 40 percent of the workers are under 30 and only one-third are 40 or over.

Farming lost out as priorities shifted elsewhere in the concern for economic progress. The number of people in farming will continue to drop and the agricultural labor force will probably continue to age. Agriculture would benefit if the labor force were shrinking parallel with a declining number of farm families and concurrent expansion of land area per family, but the decline in the farm labor force has not been accompanied by a decline in farm families. Although the farm labor force was at the prewar level by 1961, the number of farm families was then slightly under six million, not decreasing to the prewar level of 5.5 million until 1966. Farm families declined to 4,950,000 by 1975, but the rate of decrease still lagged far behind the rate in the farm labor force.

In short, men in their productive years are seeking jobs elsewhere, leaving women and older men on the farm to do the work. This fact helps explain the rising popularity of small power cultivators, which have brought the power input per unit of land above that of any other country. An increase in the number of households in which married women and older men provide the farm labor is almost inevitably accompanied by a decline in households that derive income solely from farming. Immediately after the war, the farmer had few opportunities to do anything but farm, and about half of all farm families derived their total income from agriculture. But in the ensuing years opportunities to combine agriculture with non-farm work increased, and by 1955 agriculture was the sole source of income for only 35 percent of all farmers. By 1965 almost 80 percent supplemented their income by non-farm jobs, and those for whom agriculture had become a secondary occupation had risen to 42 percent. The trend away from farming has grown stronger until at present more than 60 percent of farmers derive their chief income from a non-farming source, and only 12 percent carry on farming as their sole source of income (see Table 6). Moreover, since about one-fourth of the families in this category have no members in the productive age group of 15 to 55, the number of farmers who

Table 6   Full-time and Part-time Farming Households (percent)

Year	Full-time	Part-time	
		Income Chiefly from Farming	Income Chiefly from Non-farming
1941	41.5	37.3	21.2
1950	50.0	28.4	21.6
1955	34.8	37.7	27.5
1960	34.3	33.6	32.1
1965	21.5	36.8	41.7
1970	15.6	33.7	50.7
1975	12.4	25.4	62.1

derive their income solely from farming is probably more like 9 percent. Considering that 55 percent of farm families have no member engaged solely in farming, the majority of Japanese farm families have become virtually "non-farm" families.

Will these trends continue? Most projections made in 1970 envisioned an agricultural labor force of about 7 million, or 13 percent of the entire labor force by 1975, and 5 million or 5 percent of the total by 1985. The projections for 1975 were borne out, and although they may not hold for 1980 and beyond, there seems little reason to doubt that the farm labor force will continue to shrink. As long as present trends remain constant, the decrease in numbers of farm families will continue to be much slower than decreases in the farm labor force. Increasingly more farmers will rely more heavily on non-farming work just to make a living, and eventually all farmers will have to spend part of their time at outside jobs.

If this trend continues, it may mean a higher income and standard of living for the individual family, but if it results in more farm families whose primary sources of income are outside farming, it does not portend security for the future of Japanese agriculture. Rapid economic growth intensified imbalances between agriculture and other sectors, and if they are not resolved, we may find that agriculture has lost all options for survival, except as a hobby. Furthermore, we must find solutions soon to redirect our agriculture if we wish to prevent it from progressing into an irretrievable quagmire.

Social Change in the Village

Farm Village and Farmer in the Prewar Period

The image of the farmer before the war conjures up a work-weary soul toiling long hours under the burning sun and chilling rain barely able to coax a living out of his fields. The prewar farm village is associated with meager living conditions and backward culture, its society locked in feudal bondage. That image may be exaggerated, but there is some truth to it. Farmers were generally called *hyakushō*, a term that can be derisive today, but it was not so originally. With urbanization and development, the term *hyakushō* gathered connotations of poverty and inferior social station, and the farmer became more conspicuously an "unfortunate" member of society. Before World War II it was easy to distinguish a child from a rural area and a city child just by looking at the quality of their clothes. The ordinary farmer, barely maintaining even a low standard of living, lived a life apart from the more fortunate class of owner-farmer and landlord. It is no wonder *hyakushō* became almost synonymous with poverty. Actually, those on the lowest rungs of the urban social ladder were poorer than the farmer, and until the Taishō era the factory worker lived at a much lower standard, but the farmer struggling to make ends meet remained the symbol of poverty.

Several years before the depression, in 1926 and 1927 the Cabinet Bureau of Statistics made a survey on income which showed that poverty was the general rule in rural Japan at that time. The farm family earned on the average about seven-tenths of what the white-collar worker was making and about 95 percent of the income of the notoriously underpaid blue-collar worker. The large size of the farm family reduced rural per capita income even further. Budget figures show that half of the family income was going for food, in an ironic revelation of the farmer's difficult circumstances (see Table 7). In 1934–36 the average owner-farmer was spending 49 percent of his family budget for food, the owner-tenant was spending 52 percent, and the landless tenant 57 percent.

Table 7   Household Expenses, 1934–36 (percent)

	Food	Clothing	Utilities	Housing	Other
Farmers	50.5	9.3	4.9	6.3	29.0
Urban Workers	36.1	11.6	4.9	16.7	30.7

When Engel's coefficient reaches 50 or over, the living standard is clearly low; Japanese farmers before the war had good reason to follow the sternest of frugal ethics. Any consumption beyond the minimum necessary for subsistence was considered evil. But no matter how rigid the standards of thrift the farmer forced upon himself, his living conditions never improved. The only way to improve his lot was to raise productivity. That required pouring backbreaking manual labor into the land, but since farming then was done totally by self-employed family labor there was little incentive to conserve free manpower where possible by the use of machines. Hard work was the farmer's way of life.

Frugality and hard work were reinforced by general resignation to the gaps in life style resulting from the system of social stratification. In the rural village, the landlord had his style of life and the lowest farmer had his, and the same patterns held strong for the most part from the Tokugawa period (1603–1868) to the end of World War II. At the apex of the rural social order was the landlord, whose life style was so different that he seemed a being from another planet to farmers on the lowest rungs. If the landlord bought a radio, the tenant regarded that as something a landlord was entitled to. The owner-farmer might get a radio, too, but for the tenant, such a luxurious purchase was beyond his wildest dreams.

Elevating thrift to high virtue served to restrict the farmer in various ways; he could not spend the money required to take him out of the village except on rare occasions, and his work schedule did not allow frequent visits to the outside urban world. For centuries the village remained a universe where everyone performed a well-defined role in accordance with his social position. Local politics was the province of the landlord, while village self-government was the territory of the upper-class owner-farmer. The personality peculiar to the Japanese farmer was formed in this tiny universe, molded by village mores and wrought in response to the authority of those who moved the rural world, the landlord and the upper-class owner-farmer.

Still, the village was by no means a completely fixed, unchanging entity. The farmers worked hard and saved what they could, but after the Meiji Restoration they always faced the threat of greater poverty from the forces of spreading capitalism. The status hierarchy was established, but there were loopholes for mobility and farm families could rise and fall within its framework. The possibility of moving oneself and family up in society generated specific self-interested desires, but in the universe of the village even the slightest self-interest had to be carefully concealed; outwardly the farmer had to give priority to his obligations to other members of the community. Village society was not conducive to free competition.

As the capitalist economy and urban society developed, rural society appeared more and more starkly backward, but no attempts were made from within the rural village to overcome that backwardness. Farmers believed that they could never be anything more than what they were. Farm life was fixed, it would always be what it was, and it would always trail behind urban society. To reward his resignation and to compensate for feelings of inferiority accompanying the *hyakushō* image, the farmer was provided an ideological justification for his situation by an authority above him. This was called *nōhonshugi*.

The ideology of *nōhonshugi*, which can be translated as "agrarian fundamentalism," placed the farm at the very core of everything in the nation. This kind of thinking has been known in various forms in premodern times and was preached throughout the modern era. The modern agrarian fundamentalist claimed that although farming had been left behind in the surge of industrialization, it was a much more natural, healthy occupation than work in the city. Urban work and urban society were degrading and corrupting, and even though agriculture was hard drudgery, it was the foundation of state and society, the fertile womb from which all the people sprang forth. *Nōhonshugi* inherited, and in some cases exploited, the tradition of the feudal class system which ranked the farmer second only to the samurai. By extolling the virtues of agriculture and the farm village the ideology sought to compensate the farmer for the low standard of living and heavy labor he was forced to endure. It was clearly a retrogressive ideology that disguised the contradictions within rural society. What made it effective was the indoctrination program by the prewar government's intent to develop an imperialist state under the emperor system.

Postwar Change in Farm Life

The advantages gained by being a food producer gradually closed the gap between rural and urban living standards during World War II until the farm family was almost on a par with families who derived their income from work in other industries. For a short period after the war farm family income actually surpassed that of blue- and white-collar families, as severe food shortages throughout the nation sent many from urban areas directly to the farm villages to purchase their food.

Quickly, however, the income level of the farmer dropped below that of the non-farmer; by 1960 the farm family was making 85 percent of the white-collar family income, and 117 percent of blue-collar family income. In per capita figures farm income was only 65 percent of white-collar income, 89 percent of blue-collar, and 73 percent of the average income for all non-farm workers. Because farm income had risen above prewar levels, the Engel's coefficient had dropped to 44. But it was still higher than the coefficient of 38 for non-farm workers, which itself was higher than in the prewar period.

The urban-rural difference in standard of living shrank during the subsequent period of economic growth, less because of an increase in agricultural income per se than because of higher per family income from non-farm work. As a proportion of total family income, income from non-agricultural sources surpassed that from agriculture alone for the first time in 1963. That proportion has risen year by year, so that by 1970, only 32 percent of farmers' total income came from agricultural work, and by 1975, only 29 percent. Thus the increase in non-farm income was very rapid, one result being that in 1972 per capita farm household expenditures exceeded per capita household expenditures for all workers in the nation. By 1975, per capita farm household expenditures were 7 percent higher than the national average for workers.

A comparison of expenditures in urban and farm families shows that they are gradually converging, and that a steady annual decline in the Engel's coefficient has reduced it to 26 for farmers, which is below the national average for workers (see Table 8). The proportion spent on food is less than 30 percent, but there are two important reasons for that. First, the farm family diet contains much more grain than the urban diet, and second, farm families are forced to keep food and drink expenditures down to accommodate rising expenditures for education and entertainment. Thus the Engel's coefficient has its limitations as an indicator of standard of living, for farmers have had to make particularly great sacrifices in order to purchase durable goods.

Table 8   Household Expenses, 1975 (percent)

	Food	Clothing	Utilities	Housing	Other	(Education & Entertainment)
Farmers	26.1	9.1	3.2	12.5	49.1	(8.0)
Workers (nationwide)	30.0	10.0	3.7	10.4	45.9	(8.3)

In household goods, such as TV sets, washing machines, and refrigerators, over 90 percent of farmers now own such durable goods, a proportion comparable to that of non-farming families. In 1970, car ownership among farm families surpassed that among non-farm families, and in 1975 the rate of ownership was 42 percent for non-farm and 58 percent for farm families. The farm family probably needs an automobile more than the urban family, which has adequate public transportation at its disposal, but the prewar farmer would never have dreamed that one day farmers would own more cars than urban workers, and in almost every case would own a refrigerator. In the last ten years the rural level of consumption has increased faster than the urban. Between 1965 and 1970 the level of consumption increased in rural areas 47 percent and in urban areas, 27 percent. The same tendency continued in 1970–75, with the rate of increment at 32 percent and 14 percent respectively.

The increase in non-farm work largely explains another difference: the per capita household budget of the smallest farms, 0.5 hectare and under, is 17 percent higher than that of non-farm workers. Considering that household expenditures of the farmer with 2 hectares or more are almost equivalent to the average for all working families, the traditional image of the impoverished farmer struggling along on slightly over an acre is no longer applicable. During the period of recovery after the war, the criterion of economic power among farmers shifted from status as tenant or owner to size of farm, and now there is little relation between farm size and the living standard of the farmer. The frugal farmer closely watching his budget because his land was very small disappeared during the postwar period. The fact that these farmers, many ex-tenants, were not wed to the earth, gave impetus to their move into non-farm occupations. Farmers with stable non-farm employment throughout the year, what might be called steady part-time farmers, were 16 percent of the total in 1960; 15 years later they were 38 percent. Most of these people would have qualified in the past for any of the various nicknames given the poorest farmer such as *santan byakushō* and *gotan byakushō* (three- and five-*tan* farmers; one *tan* equals approximately one-eighth of a hectare). Farmers with 1 or 2 hectares have the most difficult time making a living, for their farms are just big enough to prevent them from taking on non-farm part-time work.

In sum, farming is no longer the chief source of livelihood for all farmers, including part-time farmers with very small plots, and the importance of non-agricultural work is increasing. Very few rural villages remain whose residents live off the land. An increasing number of people live on farms and commute to jobs in other industries, or work in other cities to return to the farm only during the busy season. Independent farmers who derive their entire living from agriculture make up only 10 percent of all farmers. For a long time the importance of increasing their numbers has been stressed, but this group remains about the same size. As the standard of living increased along with rapid growth in the economy, the farmer had to find new sources of income to catch up with those increases, which was almost impossible by raising agricultural production. It has become even more difficult in recent years because the government has been reluctant to raise the price it pays producers for rice. Overproduction has meant little profit from fruit harvests, and the dairy farmer cannot increase his income through higher prices because the supply of milk and milk products is more than adequate. The urbanization of farm life gives the farmer little alternative but to find work in some non-farm occupation if he wants additional income. During the first half of the 1960s it took at least 1.5 hectares of land for a farmer to make his living solely in agriculture. But that was 20 years ago and now a farmer must have 2.5 hectares. In the not-too-distant future, he will require even more.

The prewar farmer had at least one advantage over the urban worker: as long as he toiled on his plot of land, he had something to eat. He was able to retain this advantage by repressing any desire for other things society and culture had to offer. But those days have long passed. As the curtain closed on that era, people began to search for a richer, more varied life. Today agriculture does not give the margin for a rich cultural life. If he cannot hope to enjoy the same recreational, cultural, and educational activities and entertainment as others, the farmer will probably not get full satisfaction from his work. It is difficult to call life rewarding, or even human, when old people and women labor in the fields while the younger men commute to part-time jobs; when women come home exhausted from farm work or a low-paying factory job so the family can have cash income; or when a family is temporarily separated because the father has gone to one of the big cities to make enough to provide for his wife and children.

This is the pattern of life for the Japanese farmer as he stands at an important crossroads. Two possible directions are open, one leading to a pattern of agriculture that can by itself support farm families, the other leading to supplementary farming, which produces income used only to augment other, non-farm income. Which way farm society moves will depend, of course, on the situation of each individual farmer and farming family. It seems that most have already chosen the latter, but the farmer who derives his living solely from agriculture has yet to decide which road to take. Pressures on the rural village are pushing agriculture into the status of a subsidiary occupation. If they accept the status quo, that road may only lead to a quagmire.

Progress and Stagnation in Rural Society

World War II opened the way for great changes in the lives of farmers and rural society. A lost war snuffed out the ideology of *nōhonshugi* and its appeal to fight for Japan's future as a world power; it erased any dreams of elevating agrarian society and its values and making them the foundation and glory of the nation. With the passing of the ideology, the justification for the toil of the farmer was also lost. Even before the war the Japanese farmer knew all too well how unprofitable his vocation was, but ideology helped him to endure. When that proved impotent, he turned toward making agriculture more profitable. That effort was the chief factor behind the development of agriculture after the war. Bereft of his ideology and willing to try anything in a new effort to calculate both his and his family's labor in terms of wages, the farmer began to shift from the traditional methods, and their reliance on "knack" and intuition, to scientific, rational technology, and to mechanization.

When "democracy" replaced the values of *nōhonshugi*, the farmer could no longer settle for the particular life style allotted him, and the *hyakushō* image dimmed. Ethical sanctions on consumption as morally reprehensible and on cultural aspirations as shameful luxuries were no longer relevant in postwar society. Expectations for a better standard of living rose throughout the farming population, forming a new sense of values that encouraged efforts at raising production and making agriculture more profitable. Those farmers whose land could not turn a profit had to acquire the higher income they wanted from outside work.

The ideals of democracy and the end of the class system rather quickly stimulated new aspirations for the "better things in life" at all levels of the postwar farm village. The former tenant who at one time could not have conceived of owning a radio, now saw himself on a par with the old landlord and made plans to purchase a TV. The prewar farmer's raison d'être lay in hard work, frugality, and eternal scrimping to augment the family assets, but after the war it quickly became anachronistic to counsel restraint in buying a color TV or new car, for frugality was no longer considered to serve the best interests of the family.

The pattern for the very basic necessities of life, food, clothing, and housing, has in itself changed. When he goes to town, the farmer wears the same type of suit or sports jacket as his urban contemporary. The farm wife goes to the beauty parlor and chooses the same hairstyles as her city cousin. Diet, too, has changed drastically to include a much wider variety of flavors and seasonings beyond the commonly used *miso*, salt, and soy sauce. In houses, most notably in the kitchens, facilities are far more convenient and comfortable. Gone is the farmer's wife who bent patiently over her earthen stove, feeding in wood and blowing through a bamboo tube to fan the coals to crimson, hauling bucket after bucket of water over a heavily traveled path from well to cooking area. In 1960 only 25 percent of farm settlements had plumbing and less than 10 percent were supplied by public reservoirs. Today one-third of settlements are supplied by the public water system. The old kitchen has been remodeled and propane gas has replaced wood and charcoal. More than 60 percent of rural settlements now have running water and modern plumbing (see Table 9). This represents a remarkable change, in view of the fact that as much as 60 percent of villages 15 years earlier relied chiefly on hand pumps and buckets to draw their water supply.

Table 9   Main Sources of Drinking Water for Settlements (percent)

Year	Public Water-supply System	Private Water-supply System	Wells	Spring Water, Streams, Rainwater
1960	7.2	17.2	62.5	13.2
1975	33.2	28.6	27.1	11.1

The farm family usually had to take care of its own garbage disposal and sewage treatment, but by 1975 half of the villages either had public dumps or contracted private companies to handle those jobs. The 1975 agricultural settlement survey shows that in 27 percent of all agricultural villages, sewage disposal was being handled by a public facility, and in 17 percent, by private companies. Thus, the residents in 55 percent of rural villages were still taking care of their own sewage disposal. The major factor in the shift to public facilities and private contractors is the geographic expansion of urban political and economic jurisdiction and consequent absorption of villages into larger urban units, thus giving them access to urban facilities. It is interesting to reflect that not too long ago farmers used to go to nearby cities to collect nightsoil for use on their fields, while today they utilize the services of those cities to get rid of sewage. Fifty-one percent of the villages now leave their garbage to be picked up by public trash collectors. Did the prewar farmer ever dream that the day would come when garbage trucks would traverse their roads? The same survey indicates growth in leisure time and changes in the way it is used. Eighteen percent of rural villages have some amusement or recreational facilities and although not all were set up especially for the local people, they often use them.

Except for the Buddhist *bon* festival, Boy's Day, the Doll Festival, New Year's, or local shrine festivals, the rural family had few opportunities for recreation. Now, however, entertainments abound. Watching television is by far the most frequent, but another favorite pastime is visiting the local city. It has long been a common practice in hot spring areas for older people to go periodically to some local spa for relaxation, but this custom has now spread to other age groups. Almost 30 percent of farmers go on annual trips, stopping at least one night at an inn or hotel and spending almost as much money as urban worker families. Joining the large numbers of urban Japanese who go abroad, more and more farmers are traveling to foreign countries. The agricultural cooperative, Nōkyō, has gained certain notoriety for the numbers and sometimes less than refined behavior of the people on its tours, but it has made possible inexpensive travel abroad for many farmers who would never have the chance otherwise.

The desire for further education has grown with more free time, exposure to a wider world, and a greater variety of opportunities. No one believes today that "farmers don't need education," or fears that if one's children go to high school they will not want to take over the farm. Fifteen years ago only half the children of farmers received more than the compulsory nine years of education, but today 90 percent go on after graduating from junior high school, a higher rate than that for urban areas. New ideas and concern for the future, furthermore, have encouraged the establishment of prefectural and other training facilities for young people based on the assumption that high school alone cannot prepare a person to work in modern agriculture. This represents a virtually revolutionary change in thinking since the war.

Despite significant advances, backwardness and stagnation remain in many areas of rural society. The transition from older, rural values to urban values has been accelerated by daily contact with the urban world by commuters and farmers working part-time in the city, as well as through TV and the other mass media, but that transition has not affected rural society at a uniform rate. When urbanization reaches the agricultural village, the transplant produces imbalances that delay thoroughgoing modernization because pockets of backwardness and stagnation remain. But cultural change anywhere is always an uneven process, and Japan's villages will experience its imbalances and incongruities for some time.

Rural attitudes toward modern farm technology are today positive, aggressive, and creative, but basic values that concern the family are changing only very slowly. Parents will buy a TV set, but it does not occur to them that their child needs a desk; newlyweds take extravagant honeymoon trips, but little is done to modernize their family life. Changes are taking place in family life, but the persistence of old habits and patterns creates friction with the new, which, with no immediate solutions, produces stagnation. The old is no longer functional but it is familiar; the modern is uncomfortable and strange.

These phenomena are not limited to family life. Pockets of resistance to change become all the more visible as new developments in the economy and technology continue to affect rural society. As farming becomes increasingly a part-time occupation, rural society becomes more diverse; its homogeneity is shattered by radical structural change that cannot move all areas of society uniformly to accommodate it. For structural change can reach just so far in a given time; in many areas old, persistent traditions hold sway over the workings of rural society, becoming obstacles to progress.

Now closely linked to the urban world, the contemporary rural village can no longer sustain itself as a small self-contained universe. Commercialization and diversified, higher levels of consumption have forged strong mutual dependency between farm and city that is strengthened by the farm laborers who commute do part-time work in the city. Close rural-urban relations between village and city and new patterns of local government no longer allow rural communities to be treated simply as "agricultural society." The village is now part of autonomous local governments that incorporate many urban patterns in their operation. The rural population is thus made that much more aware of how behind the times its life environment is. Despite growth in personal consumption—or perhaps because of it—there has been little investment in social overhead in the rural village, which in turn has created other imbalances in patterns of consumption.

The village cannot exist if its population does not fully take account of national economics and politics. The direction in which rural society will move in large part depends on national policy. But farmer participation in national politics is still not strong enough to generate a promising future in rural Japan. Political participation by Japanese farmers so far has not only been weak, it has been counterproductive. More contacts, better information, a strong awareness of the workings of Japan's politics, a better grasp of his own needs, and stronger participation based on far-sighted goals are all necessary if the farmer is to benefit from the political process.

Chapter Two

Life of the Farm Family

The Prewar Family System

The Rural Ie and Patriarchal Rights

In comparison with the typical family of the West, the prewar Japanese farm family was larger in size and more complicated in membership. Marriage did not necessarily mean the beginning of a new family, but rather the entry of one more, the bride, into the husband's family. The Japanese farm family is traditionally based on the principle whereby the new couple who will inherit the farm one day lives together under the same roof with the preceding generations, the husband's parents and grandparents on his father's side. This pattern, the stem family, was overwhelmingly more common than the nuclear in rural areas and what were nuclear families in form tended to become stem-type families with the passage of time.

The stem family was the dominant pattern among all prewar families, but it was strongest and most prevalent in rural areas. Table 10 presents some findings from an analysis of a 0.1 percent sample drawn from the first national census of 1920. Clearly, the most important relationship in the family was the parent-child rather than husband-wife relationship; the stem-type family with strong patriarchal lines of succession and authority was the foundation on which Japanese rural society was built.

The family was, furthermore, more than just its members. The word *ie* describes its nature as a continuing entity, carried

Table 10   Number of Generations in a Single Household, by Occupation of Household, 1920 (per thousand)

Occupation	Number of Generations				
	1	2	3	4	5
Agriculture, forestry, and fishery	94.8	480.7	378.0	44.4	0.5
Commerce and manufacture	224.0	601.3	166.4	8.5	—
Public service and professional	325.2	499.9	166.7	8.2	—

on through patrilineal descent from generation to generation. Because of the existence of the *ie* as an entity in itself, the family at any given point is no more than the concrete manifestation of that entity. The *ie* thus embodies a continuing genealogical entity, and that allows even a single individual to represent the *ie* without creating a family group, and it also allows servants and other non-kin persons involved in the family business to be incorporated into the group through the creation of fictive kinship ties. The *ie* can be divided to produce one or more branch families (*bunke*), which then continue and function in exactly the same way as the original *ie* (*honke*), becoming an entity that is carried on by succeeding generations of male representatives.

The Japanese rural family must be understood, therefore, in terms of its place in society as an *ie*, which is an ongoing entity transcending the members of any particular family. The *ie* signified, therefore, the group of individuals who made up the family at any given time, and second, it referred to the physical house where they lived, all family possessions, the graveyard where the ancestors were buried, its fields and forest land, farm animals and tools, and everything else owned by the family. Because it was a continuing entity with property, the *ie* had its own, fixed position in the village hierarchy. The *ie* itself was accorded priority over any of its individual members, and they were, as a result, expected to sacrifice personal wishes for the sake of the *ie* if conflict should arise. Individual personality (*hitogara, jinkaku*) was less important than family pedigree, social standing, and reputation (*iegara* or *kakaku*), and family members were trained to think first of maintaining or raising the standing of the *ie* and upholding its standards and traditions. In old, wealthy landlord families in particular, a set of family precepts provided managerial and behavioral guidelines. The members were trained to defer to these precepts in honor of the ancestor who formulated them, so that the *ie* would be kept strong and flourishing. The concept of the *ie* as an entity transcending particular family members and continuing through the generations was central to the traditional family system. It was essentially a product of the particular form of feudalism that developed in Japan, but remained influential even during the modern period, most notably in rural areas.

The importance attached to the *ie* meant that the head of the house had a great deal of authority. First, he had ultimate power of decision in all matters relating to family property (property was acquired, maintained, and disposed of in the name of the *ie*, not any individual member); second, he was the central figure in family religious observances and rites held in honor of the ancestors; and, finally, he supervised all family business and directed the functions of each member as participants in the family. Thus the head of the house in rural areas held both the right of control over all *ie* assets and farm operations. He had many years of direct experience in farming, and this was an era when experience was more important than knowledge of scientific techniques. That experience enabled him to retain his rights into old age, or at least until he retired and passed them on. His farm was generally so small in size and autarchic in nature that the househead had to place the security of the *ie* before anything else, and the younger generations were not encouraged to consider or try out new techniques. Younger men worked as farm labor under the direction of their father until the eldest son succeeded to the head of the house. Wives and daughters-in-law had even less independence. They could do no more than passively take orders from the househead, and sometimes from their husbands as well.

Income from all farm labor was held by the head of the house. Even if an individual contribution could have been calculated in terms of money, no one would demand personal payment, for agriculture was a family operation that produced income from family property. The head of the house, therefore, by virtue of his control over all proceeds from farming, also regulated the consumption patterns of the family. The wife of the head received petty cash for household expenses, but no large purchases could be made by anyone without receiving permission and cash from the head of the house. Even personal pocket money was doled out to individual members only upon request to the head.

Even though house headship carried with it a great deal of authority over production and consumption, the head was not actually an absolute, authoritarian ruler of the house. His authority was seldom treated with any particular deference in the course of everyday affairs, except perhaps in some of the large established landlord families. He might be the first to bathe every evening, and he might be given saké with dinner, with an extra side dish, but generally there was little need felt to display his importance through rituals or symbolism. He was expected to take the seat of honor (*yokoza*) at the family hearth because that was reserved for the head of the house, but privileges accorded him personally were the exception.

Identical patterns prevailed among the lowest stratum of tenant farmers as well. Since the poor tenant lacked the material basis to support a strong consciousness of the *ie*, authoritarian control was exerted less heavily than in middle and upper class farm families. In poor families, poverty more than *ie* consciousness reinforced the family unit, demanding the family to work together. The individual was subsumed in this unit and for important decisions, the desires and pronouncements of the household were closely followed.

Inheritance and Family Relations

In conformity with the patrilineal structure of the family and lines of authority, inheritance was primarily a matter of succeeding to the house. Generally speaking, the eldest son succeeded as head of the family, but if there were no sons, the husband of a daughter (known as *muko-yōshi*) might assume the position. The succeeding head of the family would also take over the family property as a whole, or at least reserve priority in deciding its disposal. His siblings, for example, especially males, might receive a small portion if they had helped work the family land until then and had, thereby, contributed to the support of the family. Their portion was usually small, but enough to establish a branch family (*bunke*) while leaving enough for the stem family to continue. If younger sons found work outside agriculture, the family would give them some initial support, and daughters would be given a dowry as their share of the family property when they married and joined another family. It was also common that the daughters continued to receive occasional assistance from their own parents even after they married. But no one was ever given enough to jeopardize the future of the stem family, the original *ie*. Sometimes the stem family not only gave no assistance or property to younger children, but actually received contributions from them earned elsewhere.

Primogeniture as the central characteristic of the *ie* was molded by the feudal social order. According to Max Weber's analysis, feudal systems in the strictest sense of the term developed only in Europe and in Japan, and Japan's feudalism did give rise to an inheritance system quite different from those in China and India. While patterns of inheritance in both China and India were characterized by equal division among all agnatic relatives, in Japan the system of primogeniture inheritance spread downward from the samurai class to the common people. Its influence continued after the end of the feudal period, and it was even reinforced by the inheritance provisions of the Civil Code enacted toward the end of the nineteenth century. In the case of farm families, however, there were many exceptions to the rule of inheritance by primogeniture, and not even the ban in the Tokugawa period on the division of holdings could totally prevent the appearance of new *bunke* with land apportioned from the stem family holdings. Other variations were seen in districts where productivity was low, for example. In such areas when the eldest son was too young to inherit the family property, it was fairly common to find a husband for the eldest daughter as soon as possible to augment the family's labor force and eventually pass on to him the headship of the house, a practice called *ane-katoku* in some districts. In some other districts, where holdings were small and out-migration to the city was common, all older boys left the family and the youngest son remained to inherit, a practice called ultimogeniture. The nineteenth-century Civil Code, however, by giving legal sanction to the form of inheritance institutionalized in samurai families, insured that primogeniture would dominate inheritance patterns throughout Japan. It became even more rigidly institutionalized in farming districts where holdings were, in any case, far too small to be divided.

Under such a system, the eldest son naturally enjoyed a high status in the family. The position of the children in the farm family is summed up in the pithy maxim, "One to sell, one to follow, and one in reserve." In the ideal family a girl came first, the "one to sell," that is, to be given away in marriage. Next hoped for was a son, the heir. Finally, since no family could feel secure with only one son, another son was necessary in case the eldest should die young. The eldest son was often treated quite differently from his younger brothers, and everyone was made to understand that he was more important. This tendency was most conspicuous in the less-developed areas, especially the northeast, where the eldest son was referred to as *ani* and younger sons as *oji*. In such districts younger sons really were mere "understudies." Even in more advanced areas, the eldest son might be called *oyakata*, while the younger sons were known as *hiyameshigui* meaning literally, "eaters of cold rice," implying very low status. The intrinsic appeal of children to their parents by no means depended on the order of their birth; rather, it was a categorical imperative of the *ie* system that the heir should be given a higher status than his younger brothers. He was destined to become head of the family, but he also would have the responsibility of caring for his parents later on.

By contrast, younger sons—except in families wealthy enough to send them to middle school—would be expected to work on the family farm as soon as they finished their primary education if the family had a sufficiently large holding. This was a kind of repayment to their parents. Then, after they had finished service in the military, they would normally try to become independent. In poorer farm families without enough land to use their labor, they would go out immediately in search of work as shop assistants or factory workers or craftsmen's apprentices, in the hope that they would not only become independent, but be able to contribute to the support of their parents. In the case of upper class farm families in the less-developed districts whose holdings were large, one of the younger sons might continue to live in and work for the stem family even after marriage. A married younger son living and working with his parents was usually spoken of as "doing service" to the house which his elder brother was going to inherit. The younger son was in a position similar to the employee who worked for the family on an annual basis. Conversely, in many of the less-developed regions, employees sometimes would be set up as heads of branch families, just as the younger sons were. Relations between the household or heir and the rest of the family members were hierarchical, a feature common in the feudal era. Just the fact that younger sons were considered to be rendering service to the stem family says much about the basically unchanging aspects of the Japanese farm family since the Tokugawa period.

Daughters, on the other hand, were not necessary to preserve the *ie*, and since considerable expense was involved in arranging for their marriages, daughters were considered a burden. "A girl first" was considered fortunate only because, since girls were likely to be born anyway, one might as well come early so that she could later help with the housework and younger children. The status of girls was generally low—they were first and foremost "things to sell," that is, to marry off. Once past their marriageable age, they were called "leftovers." In a system in which men were all-important, when a daughter was married it was necessary to give her a reasonable dowry, and even after marriage her parents continued to supply some of her clothing and pocket money to help improve her position within her husband's family; hence the proverb warning that the birth of three daughters can mean the ruin of a house. Among the poorest farmers, however, a daughter had little hope of having much of anything spent on her. For such families daughters were workers who might bring in something from the pittance they earned as factory girls or maid-servants. When worse came to worst, they were quite literally sold into prostitution for the sake of their parents.

Marriage and the Status of Women

Marriage under the *ie* system concerned the two marriage partners themselves much less than the two *ie* to which they belonged. Most important was that marriage constituted a bond establishing a relationship between the two families, which meant that agreement between their respective househeads was the decisive factor. Above all, it was important that the "standing" of the two families be reasonably compatible. We find, therefore, that landlord families in the very top stratum of the village community and the poorest tenant families tended to seek marriage partners from some considerable distance because of a shortage of suitable candidates near at hand. Families in the middle strata were able to make alliances with families of more or less equal standing living not far away, but since the last quarter of the nineteenth century the degree of village endogamy has declined considerably. Thus, even in those districts where certain peer groups—the *wakamono-gumi*, or young men's groups—used to exercise some control over marriages within the village, the go-between marriage became standard as the *wakamono-gumi* gradually lost this function. Relatives or friends now take it upon themselves to search out a suitable partner for a young man or woman. This person, whose function is to bring the two together, is not always the person who plays the role of go-between at the wedding ceremony. The practice of using a ceremonial go-between (known as a *nakōdo-oya*) was institutionalized in some districts as a form of patron-client relation, which will be discussed below.

The personal character of the bride was less important than matching two families of roughly equal social standing, or, frequently preferred, finding a bride from a family slightly less wealthy than that of the groom. That, supposedly, would insure easier handling of the daughter-in-law. The second important quality in a bride, especially in middle- and lower-strata families, was her ability and willingness to work hard. Her function in very practical terms, in an established *ie*, was to produce the next heir and to supplement the family labor force. A farm woman almost literally was the "milk cow and oxen without horns." In China, just as in Japan, the ideograph 嫁 ["woman" plus "house"] was used to describe the daughter married off by a family. In China, however, the family receiving the woman used the ideograph 媳 ["woman" plus "son"], implying that she was the son's woman, while in Japan the first ideograph was retained for both outgoing and incoming brides, meaning that the family who received her considered her part of the *ie* more than the son's woman.

As a consequence, loving affection between the two partners was not of primary importance for marriage. If the head of the house or parents approved the marriage, that was enough. Gradually, the wishes of the partners came to be given some consideration with the development of the practice known as the *miai* or "mutual viewing," a carefully arranged meeting at which the prospective bride and groom were allowed to "inspect" each other. But even then it was by no means a fully mutual affair; the girl's function was simply to be seen and she had almost no opportunity at all to express her own personal wishes regarding her mariage. "Love" was considered to be on the same level as the casual mating of animals, and marriages based on it were generally thought to lead to unhappiness. "Those who come together in passion stay together in tears," goes the old proverb. The Meiji Civil Code of 1897 contained a clause stipulating parental consent for marriage up to the age of 30 for men and 25 for women, thus giving the force of law to the social custom that gave the power of decision over marriage to parents. In brief, the young bride owed obedience to the househead more than to her husband; she had to adapt herself to "the ways of the family" as a daughter-in-law rather than as a wife, and if she failed, the head of the house or her husband's parents could one-sidedly demand divorce.

A wealth of social customs remains in proverbs: "Parents are irreplaceable but brides can be changed at will," or "Brothers and sisters are as irreplaceable as hands and feet, but wives, like kimono, can be changed at will." Unless she served her mother-in-law well and was careful not to upset her husband's sisters (known as *kojūto*; literally "little mothers-in-law"), her status as bride might be hard to maintain. In many parts of Japan a form of experimental marriage known as *ashiirekon* was practiced. In any case, it was fairly rare that a marriage was recorded by entering the bride's name in the family register of her husband as soon as the marriage took place. Only after she had shown that she could fit into the family and serve her parents-in-law, or perhaps only after becoming pregnant, would her common-law status become a legalized marriage. For a girl entering a new family as a bride, the birth of a child was the first step toward achieving security in her new family.

Since the bride had no opportunity to get to know her husband before marriage there was no chance of entering marriage in a spirit of loving intimacy. So it was very difficult after marriage for her to talk to her husband freely and without reserve. Even if intimacy did develop there were severe restraints to prevent them from giving it overt expression. Her mother-in-law, who long before also gave patient and arduous service to her own husband's parents, was likely to demand the same stoic restraint from her own daughter-in-law. The relation with her mother-in-law was a source of great frustration for any young bride. Her husband was unable to provide any solace, for, given the enormous weight attached to the parent-child relationship, it was hard for him to side with his wife or to protect her from abuse by his parents. Even without such protection, if the young couple could have escaped into their own world from time to time, life might have been easier to bear, but the open structure of a typical farmhouse did not offer any privacy to the young couple. In a situation in which one could not even talk privately in bed, the bride's mental suffering was bound to be considerable.

Many brides also suffered from weariness. The young wife was the first to get up in the morning and the last to go to bed at night. In every aspect of daily life—at mealtimes and in the order of taking baths—the lowly status of the bride was always made explicit. Especially in the busy seasons of agricultural work, she often became totally exhausted. A visit to her parental home, customary at the end of a busy season, was often one of the few holidays a bride could look forward to, and an occasion that made life bearable for some. It was not only an opportunity to recoup her physical energies, but it was also a chance to relax with her own parents and brothers and sisters, and freed from the psychological pressures of her husband's family, to unwind. It also provided an occasion for her parents to give her pocket money or new clothing.

These visits home became less crucial as the bride bore children and became accustomed to life in her husband's family. Eventually her days as a "young bride" would be over. As her husband became househead, she, too, would become mistress of the household and her position would be secure. In some districts a special ceremony, known as *hera-watashi* (literally "handing over the paddle," the flat wooden utensil with which rice is served), marked the transfer of authority to the new mistress of the household, but in most districts there was a gradual and natural transition as the parents-in-law became old and unable to work. Becoming mistress was parallel to the son succeeding the father, and it meant assuming the matriarchal duties and rights of the *ie*. All household matters were now within her sphere of competence; her long years of backbreaking toil in the fields as well as in the home had earned her a status of some importance. She was still very much subordinated to her husband, however, and although one speaks of the authority of the mistress of the household, it was far inferior to that of the househead. Finally, as she grew older and reached the status of retired grandmother, or when her husband died and her son became househead, her position in the family once again declined. Now she had to take orders from the new househead, her son, and from his wife, formerly the young bride whom she had under her control.

Perhaps it was natural in such a marriage for a young mother to lavish affection on her children, for there was not always the chance to develop strong emotional feelings for her husband. This pattern was common, however, not only in farm families, and one effect of it was to make the relationship between mother and daughter-in-law even more difficult. But the children were also grandchildren, and this was a source of inconsistency in child training, for children were frequently spoiled by their grandparents. As the child grew older, however, and as the position of househead passed from his indulgent grandfather to his stricter father, implicit obedience was expected of him. To obey was the first and primary meaning of filial piety. And so the child, indulged when young, was increasingly suppressed as he grew older. Even then, the mother's unqualified affection often encouraged an *amae* (psychologically dependent) tendency in the son. In short, the low status of women in the prewar farm family adversely affected the child's personality development.

Each member of the family, if they observed the patterns of behavior expected of them according to their respective status, contributed to harmony in the *ie* as a whole, in which the head of the house was central. It was a matter of emotional unity rather than suppressed individuality. Harmony was maintained not so much by sacrificing the individual ego as by operating within a system that did not permit the ego to develop. That was true particularly of rural women.

Change in Family Life

Dissolution and Survival of the Ie

Drastic and rapid changes took place in farm family life after 1945. Before the surrender, the two important sources of pride were Japan's so-called national polity, which people saw as a unique and noble destiny for Japan in the world, and the *ie* system, which was the model for all Japanese families. After the war, the *ie* system lost its symbolic function as the repository of virtue and was instead condemned as a relic of the premodern feudal era. Article 24 of the 1946 Constitution stipulates that in "[all] matters pertaining to marriage and the family, laws shall be enacted from the standpoint of individual dignity and the essential equality of the sexes," thus establishing a perspective from which postwar social critics could lash out at the farm family as the sole survivor of the *ie* system. According to the new thinking, the farm family head had too much authority and was too strong; the relationship between the eldest son's wife and his mother was so cruel as to be almost inhuman. Adopting ideas of equal inheritance, revisions were made in the Civil Code to abolish the right of inheritance and succession to head of the house by primogeniture.

This caused much controversy at a time when rural Japan faced serious problems in having to absorb an overabundance of young men. On one hand, it was feared that equal inheritance would fragment farmland into portions too small to be viable, but at the same time, it was thought that to carry on as before, allowing the eldest son to inherit all family assets, would deprive younger children of the wherewithal to build a future. Attempts were made several times to enact special legislation to deal with inheritance of farm property, but they all failed and the provisions of the Civil Code were applied equally throughout Japan. This represented a great change from the old Civil Code, which was based on the Confucian tenets of the samurai class.

If a legal system is revised in order to effect change in living customs, and the ideals or substance of those laws are too far removed from reality, old social customs will remain intact, which is exactly what happened to the *ie* system in the early post-war period. Legal change alone did not make any immediate difference in the daily life of the farm family. In the cities, where salary and wage earners had been unable to maintain *ie* traditions for some time, the provisions of the new Civil Code were accepted with relative ease. But in the rural areas, where the *ie* system and the realities of life were still entirely congruent, it was extremely difficult to suddenly shift over to the new patterns demanded by the Code. With time, however, the general change in values among Japanese during the postwar period left its mark on the farm family, too, and by 1955 when economic growth began to undermine the bases of agriculture, there were clear signs of deterioration in the *ie* system as well.

Changes also took place in family composition. Economic limitations and the housing shortage made it difficult for each conjugal family to have its own living quarters, and so family size did not change much right after the war. In fact, in the immediate postwar period, the average number of family members increased slightly. No conspicuous decline occurred in family size until around 1955, when the economy began to move into a growth phase. In the farm family as well, the average family size remained at slightly more than 6 for the first postwar decade, but by 1960 it had dropped to 5.7, by 1965 to 5.3, in 1970 to 4.9 and in 1975 to 4.7 (see Table 11). In 1960 only 15 percent of farm families had 3 members or less, but by 1975, 26 percent fell in this category. Conversely, the majority of farm families in 1960 had 6 or more members, but by 1975 only 34 percent were that large. Reflecting the outflow of younger farm workers and the general aging of the farm labor force, in 1955 all those 40 and over in the farming population came to 29 percent of the total, and that figure rose in 1960 to 42 percent in 1970, and 47 percent in 1975. The farm population is aging much faster than the general population, which is clear when

Table 11   Change in Household Size

Year	National Average	Farm Average
1946	4.9	6.0
1950	5.0	6.1
1955	5.0	6.0
1960	4.5	5.7
1965	4.1	5.3
1970	3.7	4.9
1975	3.4	4.7

we learn, for example, that people over 65 were 8 percent of the nation's population in 1975, but they made up 14 percent of the rural population.

As family structure changed, family attitudes changed, too. The "*ie* consciousness," that set of ideas which governed the way things were run in the traditional farm family, slowly, steadily weakened. That consciousness was vitiated partly by the land reform, which uprooted the very foundations of family standing, the criteria that determined class and status divisions in the village. Now more than three decades after the reform, one finds very little trace in members of the younger generation of the status consciousness or values associated with landlord, owner-farmer, and tenant. Young people also no longer accept the need to sacrifice all personal desires for the sake of the *ie*. More important than ancestors are those living right now, and people are not avidly concerned to protect assets handed down from ancestors, to work to preserve and improve the family standing, and not so many are content to remain in the native place of their family since generations past.

Along with the steady decline in the importance attached to the *ie*, the authority of the head as representative of the house and director of its members naturally eroded. Even today the person who holds legal title and rights to the disposition of the land continues to be the middle-aged farmer or his father. Only rarely have legal rights been transferred to the successor, or son. Membership in such organizations as the Land Improvement District, the Agricultural Cooperative, or the Hamlet Association is usually in the name of the title-holder, who is also househead, but the day-to-day handling of actual farm affairs and participation in community activities are left to the successor. This pattern is particularly common among members of the agricultural practice union (*nōji jikkō kumiai*). It is symptomatic of a tendency spurred on by the advance of agricultural technology and mechanization; today, fathers who derived their own practical control over farming from experience with traditional farming methods have begun to transfer control to their sons at a much earlier age. The 1966 agriculture and forestry ministry "Survey on Attitudes toward Agricultural Management" shows that the average male farm operator assumed his duties at the age of 30.7. As there are no similar prewar surveys, comparisons cannot be made, but it is safe to assume that people taking over as operator are much younger in the postwar period.

After passing over authority and responsibility for farm operation to the eldest son, many househeads today nonetheless retain legal rights over family assets. One reason is simply to insure livelihood until the youngest child has been married and his or her marriage expenses paid. Another reason, however, is that many elder sons do not want the psychological burden of having to distribute assets to sisters and younger brothers, which they would have to do if they were the legal owners. That is only natural, for a fair and rational distribution of inheritance is almost impossible, and younger sons and daughters in effect give up their rights to inheritance.

More will be said about the various problems of inheritance later. It remains that by yielding all responsibility for operation to the eldest son, the househead loses the prerogative even in families where all income is derived from farming, although he may retain legal rights. In families with income from work outside agriculture, the father tends to lose even more authority, for if the eldest son works outside the farm, the father cannot supervise the son's labor, nor can he automatically deposit his son's income in the family coffers. When the househead also works in another industry, his status as farm manager suffers. Likewise, if a wife takes over responsibility for farm duties, her status is raised. In part-time farming families, the amount of money each member makes is known to the others, and much of it is retained by the individual. Members of the farm family no longer need to request funds from the head when required, as in prewar days.

This, of course, is another factor that has weakened the power of the househead.

As the members of farm families increasingly find part- or full-time work in other occupations, new attitudes and ways of handling money make their way into families where everyone is engaged full time in farming. Sons who live at home but commute to jobs elsewhere have exerted particularly strong influence on other family members. Financial independence has strong appeal to the sons of full-time farm families, who are less and less content to ask their fathers for money whenever they need it. They want to be paid, like their friends, on a fixed monthly basis. The adoption of a monthly pay system in a growing number of farm families thus erodes the patriarch's control over the purse even more.

The decline of the househead has also had an impact on personal relations within the family. Formerly, younger sons were considered almost useless except as a reserve if and when the eldest son should be unable to assume the duties of househead. In the first decade of the postwar period, younger sons must have envied the heir, because one of the greatest problems in agriculture during that time was finding adequate employment. Now, in most cases, younger brothers are better off than the eldest, for they have the freedom to choose an occupation and the non-farm employment market offers many possibilities. Younger sons are still expected to abandon any claim to the family assets, but the postwar Constitution guarantees certain inheritance rights. Part of the reason that farm parents are so willing to have younger brothers educated beyond junior high school is that they want to compensate for their inability to divide up the family property. The rising status of the younger sons is reflected in a higher level of education, while the education of eldest sons remains slightly below average. The constitutional guarantee of inheritance rights affects daughters also, especially at the time of marriage. Weddings have always been expensive occasions, but today the family spends that much more on their daughters in compensation for their inability to give them any household property.

The rate of disintegration in the traditional *ie* system has been accelerating in the last several years, but the *ie* itself remains. It can be seen above all in attitudes toward land. Surveys from the immediate postwar period show that about 80 percent of farmers unequivocally considered their land a family asset. More recent studies, however, show that this attitude has weakened. About 50 percent of respondents now say, at least for the record, that they regard farmland as a means of production rather than as family property handed down through the generations. If these surveys accurately reflect the thinking of farmers, there has been tremendous change in the last 30 years. It is perhaps correct to assume, however, that even these farmers regard land as an asset which guarantees a livelihood; they still feel much more strongly about land as an asset than simply a means of production. Equally significant is the nearly 50 percent of respondents who continue to affirm, as 30 years ago, that land belongs to the family. It is safe to say that agriculture in Japan remains a traditional family business, first and foremost, and an occupation only secondarily.

The conviction that the eldest son must take over the business is definitely fading, but farmers still want to know that someone will follow in their footsteps. A 1965 survey by the Ministry of Agriculture and Forestry showed that 64 percent of farmers wanted their children to take over the farm while only 7 percent did not. Attitudes toward family succession are still firm, even though the future of agriculture is not secure. It is worthy of note that when asked if they wished to be succeeded by a family member, 29 percent of farmers in general answered, "Don't know." Even more important, 26 percent of farmers in families where all income derives from agriculture answered, "Don't know." The implication in these figures is that farming as a family occupation is in jeopardy.

The results of a similar survey the following year showed that less than half of all farmers had decided on who would take over the farm. This, of course, includes families with small children, and they are the group less able than any preceding generation to speak for their children. They could not say they had found a successor, so their replies had to be negative. In 1966 several of my colleagues and I formed a group to study the steady drift away from agriculture as an occupation. Using similar questions, we made an independent survey and found that less than half the respondents were sure that one of their children would take over. About one-third replied, "Don't know." Most want one of their children to take over the farm, but children are increasingly reluctant, which has created a large gap between the hopes and expectations of the generations. In the 1975 Ministry of Agriculture and Forestry survey of self-supporting farmers and those intending to be self-supporting, 15 percent said they were having trouble finding someone to take over after them.

Establishing the succession to the farm is no longer taken for granted, and it is growing more difficult, but farming has, nonetheless, retained the features of a family calling. The foundations of the *ie* have not yet been shaken so hard that they will crumble. If farming were strictly an occupation commanding no more than professional commitment, it would make no difference to those involved whether farms remained family businesses or not. There would be no pressure on the family heir to succeed to chief farm operator as well as househead, and farming would be equally open to anyone to select as his occupation. Ideally, a person from any background should be able to farm if he wants to. To push someone to become a farmer who dislikes it just because he was born into a farm family runs counter to the ideal of occupational freedom. If a person does not like farming, he should be able to sell his land and find another job.

In contemporary Japan, however, attitudes toward farmland as a family asset and agriculture as the family vocation cannot be quickly uprooted. In abandoning the farm for the city, there is no guarantee of a better life, no assurance of a house to live in. One cannot simply leave the security of land and house that require no rent and provide a livelihood. A person will not change his situation unless he is guaranteed with certainty significant improvement for the present and the future. The house and farm, handed down through generations, help preserve the ethos of the *ie*, and nowhere is this ethos stronger than in the family of the full-time farmer whose entire income derives from agriculture.

Ironically, the tendency not to divide the property of the farm family constitutes an enormous obstacle to the Civil Code aim of abolishing the *ie* system. If inheritance were divided equally, the farm would not be able to survive, and this is what keeps the *ie* system intact and attitudes toward family assets strong. The same attitudes prevail even in families where income is derived from alternate sources, where affairs are oriented more toward the individual, or where the commitment to the *ie* is being forcibly weakened. Strong priority on preservation of family assets is also tending to break down in areas near urban centers, especially when a significant proportion of the family income is earned from non-farm employment and when the amount of land owned is small. But in all these cases, the eldest son still has the ancient responsibility for handling the family's affairs and social relationships and taking care of his parents; problems in dividing the inheritance equally among younger siblings rarely occur. A family that farms very little is reluctant even to consider selling its land, for that would mean losing a source of rice and vegetables and an asset that would help family members in their advanced years.

There are many factors at work to sustain the assumption that land is an asset of the *ie*. In another type of case, all the sons go to work in the city, leaving their elderly mother and father to cultivate a meager plot of land. Sometimes the parents will move in with their eldest son in the city and be absorbed into his family, but more often inadequate wages and poor housing conditions in urban areas bring the eldest son back to the village. There he has a house on which he does not have to pay rent and a supply of his own rice and vegetables. He will probably work part of the year at a non-farm job nearby, and eventually take charge of the family property.

Change in Attitudes toward Marriage

The declaration by farm daughters that "I don't want to marry a farmer" symbolizes the enormous change in attitudes toward marriage during the postwar years. The wish to avoid the difficult relationship with the mother-in-law, distaste for farm labor, and the bothersome social relations and obligations of the village are probably not new, but these sentiments are very widespread and only since the war have women had the option to act upon them. Parents, especially mothers, are inconsistent; on the one hand they hope their eldest son will marry a farm girl, but on the other, they want some other life for their own daughters.

It is common to hear complaints about how difficult it is for the heir in a farm family to find a suitable wife, but most eventually seem to get married. The daughter of the farm family cannot always find a salaried worker or husband with no mother to take care of. Some women still want to marry into a farm family, but they are very few. The rising position of women in general is another factor that has brought about since 1945 some totally new conditions surrounding marriage on the farm.

More and more marriages are based on love and courtship. According to a 1973 survey by the Women and Minors Bureau of the labor ministry, 33 percent of the marriages in rural areas were decided by the husband and wife. This is far below the 78 percent for couples living in urban apartment complexes, but it is still a marked change from the prewar period. In the 20–24 age group alone, however, those who chose their own partners were 63 percent in rural and 90 percent in urban areas. These figures include couples who were introduced by a third party, even though they made the final decision themselves. Of urban couples, only 5 percent had almost no courtship after the engagement was announced, but in the rural areas the proportion was 35 percent. This figure is high, but the remaining 65 percent probably dated after becoming engaged, showing that such practices are common now in rural areas as well. Today the wishes of the two people are in any case respected when marriage plans are announced. Table 12 was constructed from results obtained

Table 12   Marriage Decisions for the Family Heir (percent)

	Akita		Okayama	
	1953	1968	1953	1968
Parents should choose the bride of the house	37.5	4.3	24.1	2.8
By tradition, parents' opinion has priority	11.4	1.2	15.8	2.1
Parents should decide because they are better judges	15.9	2.9	18.0	2.1
Parents should decide, but respect the heir's wishes	19.9	31.7	27.8	33.0
Heir should decide, but respect parent's wishes	—	28.2	—	38.9
Should be left solely to the heir	13.1	29.6	9.8	18.7
Don't know; other	2.2	2.1	4.5	2.4

in surveys conducted by my colleagues and myself in Akita and Okayama in 1953 and 1968, and it shows the enormous change in thinking regarding the marriage of the family heir, especially in the recent priority on recognizing the rights and desires of the young people involved.

By its nature, any marriage through introduction entails the problem of status acceptablity for both sides, but this is no longer the decisive factor. The anticipation of receiving in a bride or daughter-in-law a "milk cow and oxen without horns" is now only a memory. The marriage which was totally arranged by the parents, in which the couple never saw each other until the wedding day, now seems quaint and exotic. It must be difficult for today's young woman even to imagine the feelings of her grandmother and mother, advised before marriage that the greatest virtue is patience and sent trembling to the house of an unknown man.

The wedding observances themselves are also quite different now. It used to be standard to have the ceremony and reception at the home of the bridegroom, but after World War II it became common practice to hold the festivities at a public hall or inn in a town or city. Ceremonies have grown more ostentatious in the last few years, and if possible are held at hotels and wedding halls. In the 1975 census people were asked where wedding ceremonies took place. In 20 percent of rural hamlets, community centers were most often used; in 17 percent, city, town, or village halls; in 5 percent, shrines or temples; and in 20 percent, private homes. In 56 percent of hamlets, other places, such as hotels and inns, were used. But even more important is that the custom of the honeymoon trip is fast becoming as common in rural marriages as in urban ones. In most instances, the newlyweds leave the day after the ceremony and reception. They perhaps go on a honeymoon trip simply because it is something of a fad, and they tend to choose hackneyed "honeymoon" spots. It is, nonetheless, significant that more and more farm couples can start their married life with a trip away from their families, to strengthen the bonds of affection and discuss their future together.

After the wedding there may be problems of adjusting to living arrangements. One can theorize that a new, independent family comes from the voluntary union of two people, but in the farm village it is still commonly expected that the woman will marry into the husband's house. Asked whether living by themselves or with parents is preferable, most young couples reply that life with parents is better. The results of a survey by the Agricultural Annuity Research Association are presented in Table 13, and those from a survey by the agriculture ministry's Agricultural Production Bureau are given in Table 14. Apart from some generational differences in the answers, respondents generally indicate a preference for living together with the entire family in the same house.

Table 13   Housing Situation for Young Couples and Their Parents, 1967 (percent)

	Actual Situation	Desired Situation	
		Farm Operator	Farm Head
Young couple live in separate dwelling or annex within family compound	7.7	18.5	28.6
Parents live in separate dwelling or annex within family compound	17.0		
Parents have own room(s) in same house	43.2	53.8	49.8
No room set aside for parents	30.5	16.0	5.5
Live separately	—	2.2	5.5
No particular preference	—	9.5	10.6
Other	1.6	—	—

Table 14   Preferences in Living Arrangements, 1973 (percent)

	Age Group		
	40–49	50–59	60–69
Prefer to live with heir from beginning of marriage	56	70	88
Prefer to live separately until parents can no longer work	41	27	10
Prefer to live separately on a permanent basis	3	3	2

In the last few years, however, attitudes have shown slight signs of changing to favor the position of a new couple as an independent, nuclear family. Thus we are beginning to see occasional cases when separate living quarters are set aside for the young couple, and we will probably see more of this pattern from now on. Rural houses are bigger and more open than those in the city. Traditionally they have abundant floor space and more rooms, but rarely has any area of the house been reserved for exclusive use by couples in each generation. Recently farm couples seem more in favor of building an annex onto the main house or renovating an outside farm building expressly for the use of the newlyweds. The 1966 survey by the Ministry of Agriculture and Forestry shows that 57 percent of all family heirs at that time were hoping to remodel their homes to make an area of their own for their immediate family. They did not consider separate quarters as a mandatory precondition for marriage; they simply "wanted" to remodel before welcoming their new partner. Of all the options given in the survey to improve the household environment, by far the greatest number of young heirs chose "remodeling."

Today's farm wife can look forward to a much better married life than her mother or grandmother. In the past, a young wife had to obey her mother-in-law in everything, and the mother-in-law retained the "right" to torment her daughter-in-law unrestrained. Today, the husband's mother is more likely to defer to the young wife's wishes. The frustrations of getting along with mother- and sisters-in-law are less trying today, with the help of privacy offered by their own quarters. A woman was once able to release her physical and mental tension only on occasional visits to her parent's house, but today fatigue and frustration can be dispelled to some extent at home. Greater privacy also means a healthier marital life. If the difficulty in finding a bride for the heir forces the family to renovate the house, that is in the long run a small price for a double benefit. The wife's stronger position is also a definite support for the personality development of her children as well.

Even more difficult in a family which has only daughters is to ensure that the husband of one will live with her family to become its heir. Many farm families are compelled to adopt an heir if the family wants to continue as an agricultural unit. This did not become a serious problem until employment opportunities for younger sons opened up after the war. Before that, candidates were plentiful. The old adage "If you have even three rice husks left, don't be adopted" suggests the ignominy and undesirability of a man's formal adoption into a farm family, but even that was the better of several evils for the younger sons.

Today all boys, including the eldest, can go into non-farm work as soon as they graduate if they wish and most would be reluctant to enter a family where they would have to farm full time. If the adopting family lives within commuting distance to the young man's job, and the wife, mother, and father agree to carry on the farming themselves (so-called *san-chan nōgyō*), he may accept the offer. But finding a good candidate is difficult if the adoptee has to become a full-time farmer. The attractive, intelligent woman who will give up the rights to succession of farm and house will have little problem in marrying whomever she wants. But, if she is not so fortunate, she may have to marry someone who is less than desirable, and her married life will probably suffer. Such women are also victims of the *ie* system. There is no significant protest by eldest daughters against traditional pressures. For one thing, she has the advantage of staying in her family home and avoiding the psychological stress of conflict with her mother-in-law. But as things stand now her disadvantages are perhaps greater. Ideally, she could marry the eldest son of a nearby family and amalgamate farm holdings and work, but the *ie* consciousness is still too strongly rooted to permit that, except in rare cases.

Inheritance and Post-Retirement Security

Few substantive changes have taken place in the inheritance of agricultural assets by succeeding generations. To counteract the possibility of subdivision permitted by the equal inheritance principle in the 1947 revision of the Civil Code, several attempts were made to enact mitigating laws, but none were successful. Farmers need not have worried. In 1951, the Japan Association of Private Law made a study of 241 farm households and found that only 4 had made provisions for equal inheritance. In all the others, the sisters and younger brothers had agreed to surrender their inheritance and leave the care of the parents in old age to the eldest son. In the years since that survey, there has been no basic change in inheritance patterns. The

Table 15　Farmland Inheritance (percent)

	1962	1968	1973–74
Passed on to a single heir	66.0	81.3	72.8
Divided among children	12.8	11.0	17.0
Not yet decided	14.0	4.0	7.5
No farmland to pass on	7.3	3.8	2.8

tendency to compensate younger children with cash or some other form of payment is growing, but few attempts are made to divide the land itself. Subdivision of land does take place, but chiefly in farms close to cities where land values are very high. Table 15 is compiled from survey results obtained by the Farm Inheritance Study Group and the Agricultural Policy Research Committee. It shows that since 1962 more than 10 percent of farm families have been dividing the inheritance of land assets. Most families try to keep their holdings intact, but when sub-dividing is unavoidable they devise methods to operate the farm as one unit. It is likely that children will increasingly demand subdivision of farmland in the future, especially when it can bring in income from non-agricultural use. This is not yet a serious problem, and special laws to discourage subdivision by inheritance were not necessary in the past. Such legislation would only have served to keep the *ie* system intact. But it now seems imperative that if we wish to maintain Japan's agricultural land, we must adopt the appropriate legal restraints on subdivision through inheritance, and do so quickly.

In this connection, what is called familial agreement farming, usually involving contracts between the son and parents or father, merits our attention. Such contracts originally arose not in relation to inheritance practices, but out of the need for assurances that the eldest son would continue the family vocation. As they stand now, they will not solve inheritance problems, but they do have potential.

The biggest headache for the farm family remains the problems of a successor. Some time ago, young heirs would not take over the farm unless they had power tillers to work with. Later the parents had to buy them motorcycles, and now the demands have escalated to include automobiles, and even these accouterments no longer satisfy the farm heir. Now, unless he can be guaranteed some sort of salary payment, the successor often chooses to leave agriculture.

Father-son contracts represented an initial attempt to keep the eldest son in agriculture and to develop within him a positive commitment to farming. Contracts of this sort were first formalized in several towns and villages about 15 years ago modeled on the parent-child contracts concluded in Europe and the United States. Their inception in Japan was greeted with wide interest. The National Chamber of Agriculture set up a Council on Labor Shortage which sought to promote the use of these contracts throughout the country, chiefly as an instrument for stabilizing the labor force.

Contracts take a variety of forms, but the most popular stipulate a fixed allowance or a fixed wage, or they establish the son's management responsibility for certain activities, the income from which is his alone. Contracts providing for a fixed percentage of family income to the son are also popular. One proposed type combines wage payment with inheritance, and it stipulates that a fixed portion of the contracted wages be put into savings for the son which he will eventually use to purchase family assets. This agreement has been devised, however, more to help the parents who are unable to pay standard wages, so that they can transfer family assets to the eldest son in the form of debt payment or deferred payment.

The Japanese parent-son contract, although modeled after Western patterns, was adopted here in the interests of keeping the eldest son in farming, a function it still performs. But the Western type is based on the principle of equal inheritance. If the eldest son works with his parents on the farm and never receives any payment for his labor, it is considered unfair after the parents die to be forced to divide up the legacy with his brothers and sisters who have had nothing to do with maintaining the farm. In the equal inheritance system, the son who will eventually take over the farm receives a monthly stipend from his parents. When he gets married, he lives in a house apart from his mother and father, and after they retire he pays them rent for the farmland. With money left over he purchases the assets of the parents little by little. When they die, that which the son did not buy is divided equally among all children. If he cannot pay all the money at once, he makes an agreement to pay in yearly installments. Thus he is able to carry on the agricultural unit inherited from his parents.

The basic nature of parent-child contracts, so closely bound up with concepts of equal inheritance, is far from being adequately understood in Japan. Until the farm family has developed to the stage where it can carry out the principle of equal inheritance, it will continue to regard the surrender of rights to family assets by all but the eldest son as natural. But, as Table 16 shows,

Table 16 Attitudes on Primogeniture (percent)

	Akita		Okayama	
	1953	1968	1953	1968
Taken for granted	61.6	27.6	33.0	11.5
Dictated by custom	9.5	13.6	17.2	8.7
Cannot be helped	9.8	9.6	8.4	6.6
Any single heir acceptable	4.4	31.3	13.2	36.5
Will divide among children according to their circumstances	5.4	12.2	10.7	24.7
Prefer equal inheritance	4.4	4.3	15.0	8.3
Don't know; other	4.9	4.1	2.5	3.7

attitudes toward inheritance are changing. In 1953, there were big differences in thinking between Akita, a mountainous rice-growing region, and Okayama, where fruit orchards take up a great portion of the agricultural land. In neither area do realities allow equal inheritance. But by 1968 definite signs had appeared that the tradition of handing everything over to the eldest son was being threatened. In future generations, the demand for equal inheritance will grow and the day will eventually come when inheritance practices will truly accord with the spirit of the father-son contract. But if a special law on the inheritance of farm family assets is ever devised, the limits of Japanese agriculture will first have to be overcome. There are very few farms economically productive enough to allow the heir to maintain farming operations and pay yearly installments to his brothers and sisters.

Aside from the question of the limits of space and productivity in Japanese agriculture, father-son contracts are bound to affect farming in various ways. According to the agriculture ministry's

1966 survey of farmer attitudes, only 47 percent of family heirs had heard of these agreements and less than 1 percent had concluded a contract. Even though contractual farming, devised as a way to keep the heir on the farm, is still undeveloped, it seems certain that such agreements, beginning with fixing an allowance, will become more popular and more diverse. The ministry's 1965 survey showed that 10 percent of farmers were handing over part of the farm duties to their heirs. Considering that only 24 percent of the farm families have heirs who are presently working on the farm, this is very high. Thus, it is quite possible that well over 1 percent of the families have some kind of de facto agreement, and such practices will lead to a more strict definition of the relationships and rights of the children and will strengthen the position of the young husband and wife living in a two-generation family.

As personal relationships in the farm family become more contractual, the way will open for a system of equal inheritance. When Japanese farmers begin to realize that the current mode of agriculture itself impedes such a system, they will develop a more positive outlook on equal inheritance. That change is already taking place, as Table 16 shows. The diehard belief that the eldest or adopted son should take over the farm is fast receding. Some time in the future it will be commonplace for any of the children to succeed to the headship of the family, signaling the time when the *ie* system can be overhauled.

Problems of succession also relate to care of aging parents and old-age security. The Farm Annuity Research Association for some time has been looking into the question of how people are taken care of after they retire. According to a poll it took in 1967 of former male farm operators over the age of sixty, 84 percent were receiving support money only from their heirs. Eleven percent were earning their own livelihood. Three percent received contributions from other children as well as the heir. In only 0.5 percent of the cases were these expenses divided equally among the children.

Some respondents had given partial control to the heir when he assumed the position of farm operator, but the majority of fathers retained total control over family property. Many older people seem to believe that maintaining their rights until death will guarantee support from the children; "No one is as miserable and lonely as the old man who no longer has control of the purse strings."

Heirs themselves do not often question their responsibility with regard to parents. In the survey, 83 percent said they assumed that the heir should be the sole supporter of the mother and father. Eight percent answered that other brothers and sisters should help, even if only a little. Less than 2 percent said that responsibility for support should be divided equally among the children. Answers like these show that the *ie* tradition calling for the eldest son to take full responsibility for his retired parents is still vigorous. When asked to cite reasons for supporting the system, respondents said that such practices symbolize filial affection, and that this is the way it has been done for centuries.

But when successors were asked how they thought older people should be supported in the future, many suggested funding from personal savings and national pensions. There are bound to be dramatic changes in the present system whereby all support comes from the heir, for three reasons: it has been more than fifteen years since the national pension system was started and people in the ten-year pension group are already receiving money; almost everyone in the nation is fully aware that a pension system is in operation; and, finally, traditional systems and customs of farm life are rapidly changing. A 1973 survey by the agriculture ministry's Agricultural Production Bureau (Table 17) sheds light on some of the changes in attitude. Of people in their sixties, 77 percent, as opposed to only 22 percent of those in their forties, replied that they would rely on the family heir for support. Almost no one in his sixties said he would ob-

Table 17　Financial Support for Old Age, 1973 (percent)

| | Age Group | | |
	40–49	50–59	60–69
Will depend on pension and savings	63	20	1
Will rely on heir	22	48	77
Will retain all or part of right to assets until death	8	19	16
Expect children to take care of all or part of living expenses	6	13	6

tain financial support in old age from savings and national pension, but 63 percent of those in their forties replied that such sources would provide support after retirement.

Revisions in the national pension system in 1969 raised the monthly benefits for a retired husband and wife slightly, and in the following year a pension system for farmers was instituted, but it will be some time before those benefits are substantial enough to make any real difference. One could not begin to live on the amounts now provided. Social security standards in Japan are far below those of the Western European countries, and it is worse in rural than in urban areas. As more and more farmers take on jobs outside agriculture, the requirement that their nonfarm employers enter them in the welfare pension program has meant that many more farmers receive benefits. The amount being paid into social security programs for farm people is now almost as high as for urban workers. Calculated by household, the farm family puts about 90 percent of what the urban family pays into social security, but in per capita terms the amount drops to slightly more than 70 percent. Benefits, including those for medical expenses, are still very inadequate, and the national pension plan has just begun to pay benefits to farmers per se, so the gap between rural and urban social security levels becomes even bigger.

If changes in the life style of farmers are to be positive, improvements are needed in the social security system. Japan's farm population is already markedly older than the average urban population, and if it ages further without accommodation by the social security system, the problems of senior citizens will become all the more acute in rural areas.

Few observers in the postwar recovery period, much less before the war, could have envisioned the vast changes in farm life and living standards of the past two and a half decades. Not even the postwar revisions of the Civil Code, rising dissatisfaction with the premodern nature of the farm family, or movements for better living conditions prepared people for the present state of disarray in the *ie* system. There were very few deep changes until the mid-fifties, when rapid economic growth began, eventually producing significant changes in agriculture and farm family life. External rather than internal factors are thus responsible for the rents in the fabric of Japanese farm life. Economic growth drew young and middle-aged men away from the farm, leaving agriculture to the elderly and the women. Women, in particular, shouldered a heavy burden and, furthermore, were often forced to work part-time in local factories or other outside jobs in order to augment the inadequate farm income. The farm family has to make intense efforts to obtain cash income, which often sacrifices good family relations. More threatening to family solidarity are the long periods of absence of young men who have to go off to find jobs in distant cities.

The *ie* system may be slowly disintegrating, but farmers are not yet free of it. Only when the Japanese farm family can lead the kind of life envisioned in the Civil Code will it be truly liberated from "feudal" structures. But the marks of the *ie* are still visible in every facet of farm life. Several conditions will have to be met in order to completely eliminate the remnants of the *ie* from the farm. Farmers will have to separate their consumption patterns from farm operation and adopt corporate accounting methods. Farming must be abolished as a family business, and it must become an occupation which its workers freely choose. The eldest son who dislikes farming must be allowed the freedom to choose whatever work he wants, and he should be excused from the duties of headship if he wishes. Farmers must be able to obtain adequate income in non-farm occupations and be able to move freely without having to worry about poor housing in the cities. After retiring, the farmer must receive enough in social security benefits to enable him to live comfortably without having to take recourse to farming. The family heir must freely choose farming, and when he marries he and his wife should live apart from the parents. The heir would pay rent for the use of farm assets, eventually buying them from his parents. Family assets not purchased would be distributed equally among all the children after the death of the parents.

Contemporary Japanese rural society is not amenable to such clear-cut, impersonal conditions, and prospects for complete abolition of the system surrounding the *ie* are not good. Very few farm families use corporate accounting methods and non-farm industries do not pay sufficient wages for a farmer to live on his non-farm income alone. The government's failure to institute any kind of land policy restricting land sales and acquisition has allowed land prices to skyrocket, and the government housing policy is also inconsistent, unbalanced, and has too many loopholes. It will be a long time before farmers stop thinking of their land as a family asset, and before old-age security is gained through social security guarantees for a minimum standard of living and money saved from the farmer's own labor, instead of by handing over assets to the eldest son.

To allow the *ie* system to be totally dismantled, a great many more people will have to leave agriculture, significantly reducing the number of farm families. Even then, those remaining would not have enough land for profitable farming. They would have to adopt methods of cooperative land use or other means in order to rationalize agriculture. Prospects for cooperative farming are not very promising, which lends support to the speculation that the *ie* system will survive. Younger sons' demands for their share of inheritance will increase, if gradually, exerting pressure on the household finance of the farm family. The eldest son will be all the more reluctant to take over the farming, even though he has no alternative but to endure the agony of the *ie* system. If even then there is no widespread reaction and if generalized efforts are not made to change the political and economic status quo in agriculture, the *ie* will remain, no matter what changes come to individual farms.

Kinship Groups

Solidarity of Dōzoku

Kinship relations between families ramify as each succeeding generation creates affinal links with other families through marriage, and the family units branch off. If families live and work in proximity to each other, they form kinship groups. Mutual assistance is especially important to small farmers with limited land, who would have a hard time making a living solely on their own. It is kin relations to whom they turn, whether on an equal, reciprocal basis, or as a weaker, poorer unit which must depend on the economic strength of someone wealthier than they.

In the rural villages, such kinship groups are usually based on patrilineal descent. Unlike India and China, marriage within these patrilineal groups—indeed, until recently, within a given hamlet—was not prohibited in Japan, which resulted in considerable bilineality in families. As will be discussed later, however, even the closest affinal relations generally were overshadowed by the patrilineal descent groups. These kinship groups were broadly called *dōzoku* or *dōzokudan*, although there are also terms peculiar to a given region that refer to the same patrilineal kinship group.

A *dōzoku* is formed of a stem family plus a number of branch families, all of which consciously acknowledge their lineal and lateral relationships to each other and to the stem. A *dōzoku* is created when one *ie* divides and sets up a branch *ie* by granting the new *ie* a house and enough land for it to become independent; still, the new branch *ie* continues to recognize the stem family's ritual functions in paying honor to the ancestors or in the worship of the common deity of the *dōzoku*, and it agrees to uphold all practices and customs that symbolize ties between those of inferior and superior lineage. A *dōzokudan* cannot come into being if the branch is not given such an apportionment of family property, or if it refuses to abide by the prescribed pattern of social relations. Then it is simply a division that does not produce a bona fide branch *ie*. Interestingly, the common recognition of fictive kin relations makes it possible for servants to be set up as independent branches and therefore part of the *dōzoku* group. Similarly, if a younger son of a branch family should go to live in the stem family, sometimes as a servant, and later receive a grant from the stem family to establish himself independently, his own family joins the *dōzokudan* not as a branch of his father's house, but as an immediate branch of the stem family, with status equivalent to that of his original household. In China, the extended family was formed on the basis of strict patrilineality and equal inheritance. In the Chinese family system there never developed the kind of superior-subordinate relations that were the norm in Japan, nor were household employees ever established as their own branch family. *Dōzoku* connotes a familistic solidarity peculiar to Japan; the word is confined to those groups which are closely bound economically and emotionally and in which the boundaries of relations are clearly understood by all members.

The nature of the *dōzoku* is best understood if we examine the practical forms of family fission by which they came into being. We have already touched upon the policy during the Tokugawa period restricting excessive subdivision of land in order to ensure adequate rice for taxes, thus inhibiting free establishment of branch families. But branches were in fact established, although sometimes with difficulty, mainly because land continued to be reclaimed and because *ie* died out from time to time. After 1870 all restrictions on the creation of branch families were lifted, but even then without expansion of land by reclamation or more productive irrigation methods, a new branch was by no means simple to set up. It was possible only in families that had acquired enough land to be able to relinquish a portion for another independent family without itself suffering in social or economic status. Families that set up several branch families and held them together in a *dōzoku* were therefore nearly always large landowning families.

The position accorded the patrilineal stem family, based on continuing primogeniture, and the need to maintain its social standing meant that it retained by far the greater portion of family land. It was common in the more remote villages of the northeast for younger sons to stay with their parents for some ten years or more after marriage, and then to receive just enough land to live on. This period after marriage was one of service to the stem family. Any land or property they eventually received was at once a reward for service and an *on* (blessing), bestowed upon it by the stem family. Here we find both the origin and raison d'être of the master-servant relationship which develops between stem and branch families. Of course, this very relationship made possible the natural emergence of non-kin branch *ie* established for servants as a feature of kinship groups. Unless the stem family were very wealthy, such branches rarely received enough property to allow full independence, and even then, servant branch families usually received a smaller apportionment than genuine kin branches. It was usually necessary therefore for servant branches to continue to depend on the stem family. Thus they continued to receive stem family protection.

As tenants on the land, they were thoroughly integrated into the production system of the main *ie* and they continued to provide personal services to it.

As the process of branching continued, gradually the *dōzoku* took on a pyramidal structure, normally with an original stem family (*sōhonke*) at the top, and stem families (from the original stem family's point of view, branch families) in the middle, and finally branch families ("grandchild-branch-families") coming last. Ranking within the *dōzoku* depended on the antiquity of branching and on its lineal relationship to the original stem family. In many cases this ranking was supported by differences in real economic power and reflected in landlord-tenant relationships; in such instances original *ie* could exert effective control over the rest of the *dōzokudan*. In the Chinese pattern, clan property held in common served to unite the group, while in Japan the family property of the stem family constituted the material basis for solidarity. In the typical Japanese case the original stem *ie* maintained control over agricultural activities, weddings and funerals, building of houses or rethatching roofs, and other activities of daily life. These were carried out with the cooperation and mutual help of all members of the group. Worship of the *dōzoku* deity and its ancestors was directed by the stem family, and at New Year's and the summer festival, branch families paid formal respects to the stem family. When the authority and control exerted by the stem family was at its peak, its wishes in all matters of marriage and education were obeyed. In one symbolic representation of stem family authority, when the patriarch visited a branch family he would automatically be offered the *yokoza* rather than a *kyakuza* (guest's seat). When the *dōzoku* held a very powerful position in the hamlet and the original stem family had large landholdings, it was not unusual for families with no original relationship to the *dōzoku* to be "commended" branch families and thus be incorporated into it.

Such overwhelmingly powerful *dōzokudan* were by no means typical; they emerged only in less-developed areas. Even when such a pattern was found in the villages of a given district, it rarely followed the archetypical hierarchy of original stem, later stem, and branch families in an orderly way. In time, ranking based on descent and on economic standing normally ceased to coincide. If the original stem family declined, one of its branches might become the strongest, in which case it created its own *dōzoku* with its own immediate branch families. Then the original stem family, supported by only a few direct branches, gradually lost its position. The original stem family might even leave the village if it declined too far, and then the *dōzoku* would split up into two or more separate groups.

During the first decades of the twentieth century, holdings directly cultivated by stem families which had been very large landowners were much reduced, even in the least developed areas, which eliminated part of the need for the labor organization of the *dōzokudan* as a whole. The break-up of the *dōzoku* frequently was accelerated by this loss of function. When that happened, the unity of the *dōzoku* was maintained largely through the shared observance of certain rituals and the continuation of authority of the original stem family, to which the branches could always turn in times of need. Furthermore, a reduced area for direct cultivation meant that there were fewer live-in servants eventually to be set up in servant branch families. That meant, in turn, the gradual refinement of the *dōzoku* into a patrilineal descent group in a more pure sense, and the fading of the master-servant dimension of relationships.

In more economically advanced areas, such master-servant relationships never developed very far, if at all. The heir usually received more family property than the branch families in these areas as well, for his financial, social, ritual, and family responsibilities were greater, as we have seen, than those of other members. But in many areas younger sons established branch families soon after marriage, which were not necessarily in a subordinate position to the stem family. If they did not have enough land to become independent farmers, they usually took a side job. Landlords in such districts tended to become parasitic non-cultivators, and a good many of them actually lived elsewhere. Consequently, servant branch families did not appear and the *dōzoku* pattern described above did not emerge.

Even in the more advanced areas, however, the higher authority of the stem family was recognized and the characteristics of the classic *dozōkudan* persisted, although in modified from. The bonds of the *dōzoku* were maintained in agricultural cooperation and in the observance of family rituals, and in emergencies the group rallied around the stem family. The archetypical *dōzoku* described above was a basic pattern, in theory, if not always in fact, in modern Japan. Although not universal, it was certainly the most prevalent when the ranking determined by the stem-branch descent structure coincided with economic ranking. Even if there was no connection between stem and branch families based on protection and service, the branch families were in general not equal in social status to the stem families and had to defer to them. Though in everyday life there might not be dependence, when circumstances became pressing, the branch families were usually forced to turn to the economically more solid stem family.

Familistic Social Relationships

In rural society during prewar times, the importance of the *ie* far overwhelmed that of the individual members of which it was composed, and the family unit was predominant in all social relations. The structure of the *dōzoku* group was, in a sense, an extension of the *ie*. The word that most succinctly describes the nature of the *dōzoku* is familism, and Japanese familism is distinctive in that it is based both on the solidarity between parent and child and on the bonds between superior and subordinate.

Japanese familism can also be called feudalistic familism, as demonstrated most typically in the *dōzoku* groups. Social relations of the *dōzoku* type were a part of life in every farm village, although of varying strength depending on the region. Of all social relations, the most important were those between the *oyakata* and *kokata* or between *oyabun* and *kobun*.

The word *oyako* has a much broader implication than its literal meaning of "parent and child." *Oya* was sometimes equivalent in meaning to stem family, and in general the farmers with extremely small holdings whose livelihood was by no means guaranteed looked for security not to their "parent" in the kinship structure, but to the *oya* in the *dōzoku* group. Thus farming families sought *oyakata* or *oyabun* relationships even when there was no blood relation—or if there was, often to strengthen it—thus creating fictitious "parent-child" relationships. These *oyakonari* were of various kinds, such as the *nazuke-oya,* or godfather *oya,* or the *eboshi-oya, o-haguro-oya,* or *nakōdo-oya* who presided over coming-of-age, engagement, or wedding ceremonies for young adults. Once such a relationship was formed, the *oya* extended protection to the younger person as he would his last-born child, and this *kobun* would serve the *oyakata* as he would a parent, even after the death of the former. *Oyakata* were traditionally power-ful landowners or heads of stem families. *Kobun* were members of both kin and non-kin branch families, but might also come from a totally unrelated line of descent. When the "child" came from a branch family, the *oyakata-kokata* relationship overlapped with the stem family–branch family relationship. In other cases, al-though the *ko* belonged to a separate *dōzoku,* he would become dependent on the *dōzoku* of the *oya.* What I shall deal with here concerning the *oyakata-kokata* relationship is the familistic social relations which were thus created that went beyond the *dōzoku* structure.

The *oyako* relationship above all involved specific individuals. It was not a relationship between stem and branch families, nor was it created when a new family became a branch member of the *dōzokudan* subordinate to the stem. On the other hand, while in theory the *oyakata-kokata* relationship was established between two individuals, in practice the in-dividual was never considered apart from the family and so the relationship became in substance one between *ie.* Ordinarily one chose his *oyakata* from the same *ie* as had his father, making the relationship, in many cases, practically hereditary. In certain in-stances when the *oyakata* of the father and the son were from two different *ie,* then the *oyako* relationship was clearly not parallel with stem-branch relations. The reasons were usually practical. It did not mean that the *kokata* deliberately changed the family from which he chose his *oyakata,* but rather that the prospective *oyakata* himself refused on grounds of inadequate economic power to be able to sustain the relationship, or that he was too young to undertake the responsibility.

This *oyakata-kokata* bond in its strongest form developed within the mountain villages of Yamanashi Prefecture. In the area, the patronage of the *oyakata* was so overwhelming that the *kokata* was forced into a position of total subservience. When a person took on the duties of *nakōdo-oya*, thus becoming an *oyakata*, he was responsible for the *kokata* not only on special occasions such as births, marriages, and deaths, but in everyday affairs as well. The *kokata* was obliged to present the traditional gifts in midsummer and at New Year's and to render him service on a regular basis. In return, the *oyakata* was expected to give more than he received. For this reason, the *kokata* felt a debt of gratitude to the *oyakata* for his benevolence and obeyed his will in everything. The areas where such strong relationships prevailed were of course limited, but *oyakata-kokata* relations of some sort were common to all rural villages.

Inevitably, these *oyakata-kokata* relationships gradually weakened. A single *oyakata* might have many *kokata* among whom the most powerful might, in turn, have their own *kokata*. Even in regions where the *oyakata-kokata* bond was a form of control over the social relationships in the villages, they eventually lost their former force. In time the rationalism of the capitalist money economy penetrated rural areas. *Oya* landlords began to invest their money outside the local area, reducing the size of their directly cultivated holdings and becoming more and more parasitic as well as ceasing to extend the former degree of familial assistance and closeness to the *kokata* who were their tenants. On the part of the *kokata* as well, as education spread he had no more need to depend on the landlord to read and write letters or documents, and as economic conditions improved he was not forced to borrow clothing or eating utensils for special occasions. But while the degree of dependence decreased, the *oyakata-kokata* relationship continued to exist. Although in form this relationship was a bond between two individuals, it was not limited to one generation, and often assumed a hereditary character; as such it could not be expected to fade away altogether.

Even in regions which did not have the custom of taking an *oyakata*, tenants frequented the house of the landlord, bringing their rent rice and helping with various household and agricultural tasks. The houses they "frequented" (*deiri*) coincided with the stem family household in the stem-branch relationship and the *oyakata-kokata* aspect of the relationship was often the more emphasized. The scope of these *deiri* relationships, except in the case of large landowners, was restricted to a small area and only a few families, and they were also clearly of the *oyakata-kokata* type. As landlords grew increasingly parasitic on the land, these *deiri* relationships were even further reduced. Slowly the master-servant aspect of the relationship began to atrophy until it applied only to those households whose role was that of overseer and rent-collector.

In the wake of the land reform program after World War II, all these types of relationships—the stem-branch family, *oyakata-kokata* and *deiri* bonds—began to break up, but they were the core of the familial social structure of Japanese villages. These relationships were transformed as the landlord system changed, but the social relationships involved in the landlord-tenant relationship remained the important base of Japan's rural society until the landlord system itself disappeared.

Affinal Relationships and the Dissolution of Familism

The familistic bonds of solidarity of the *oyakata-kokata* and *dōzoku* began to weaken with the institution of the postwar land reform. By removing the material foundation of the *dōzoku*, the reform spelled the inevitable demise of the internal *oyakata-kokata* relationships. The landlord-tenant relationship between stem and branch families and between *oyakata* and *kokata* was almost totally obliterated. Their tenant lands taken away, stem families no longer had the economic power either to protect or to subordinate branch families. Branch families now owned their own land and were therefore freed from dependence, subordination, and the duty to serve the stem family. Even in areas where *oyakata-kokata* conventions remained strong, the *oyakata* were economically unable to assist or protect the *kokata* even if so requested.

Though the material foundation of the *oyakata-kokata* relationship was lost, the social conventions or outward manifestations remained. The branch family could not put an immediate end to its centuries-old participation in the rituals and traditions of the stem family, yet without its former economic strength, the stem family was hard pressed to respond as custom demanded. As time went on, the branch family simplified its methods of participation in such rites and rituals. In many areas, the very old practice of taking an *oyakata* continued, but mostly as a convenience to serve as go-between in marriages. Even this role became more perfunctory in nature until it was limited only to the wedding ceremony itself. As younger generations took over the headship of the family, even these ritual roles were simplified and in some instances they ceased altogether. With rapid economic growth, the *oyakata-kokata* and stem-branch relationships have almost completely faded from the scene.

This should, however, not be construed to mean that members of the *dōzoku* no longer cooperate in agricultural production; rather, when they do, it is more likely to be because they are brothers or relatives of some kind, or because they are neighbors. The sphere of cooperation has grown smaller and in most instances is restricted to exchange of labor among only two or three families. The 1955 Survey of Farming Settlements showed that traditional customs of labor exchange and cooperative work known as *yui*, *temagae*, and *tetsudai* continued in 84 percent of the surveyed villages as mutual assistance on a purely individual basis. At that time only 12 percent continued cooperative labor customs centered around a stem family or *oyakata*. Today, more than 20 years later, these traditional practices are all but extinct.

As previously mentioned, the common practice of consulting the stem family concerning the engagement and marriage of children of the branch family has also lapsed. Once a unit within the *dōzoku*, the farming household now has far more independence. But if the branch family has financial difficulties, it cannot go to the stem family for assistance, and if the stem family is threatened with collapse, it cannot be rescued by support from branch families.

This trend had actually begun before World War II; its pace was merely accelerated by the events after 1945. After the beginning of the Meiji era, it became more difficult to set up branch families, and, following the war, even harder. In the immediate postwar years, farm families kept younger sons on the land and made them heads of branch families, but the practice stopped soon thereafter and very few branch families have been founded through partition of farmland. The practice still exists today, although in most cases it consists merely of providing land or a house for a son working in a non-farming occupation.

The distribution of farmlands to a newly founded branch family is very rare, the only exception being when part-time farm families in and near urban areas divide land among branches to allow them to grow their own vegetables and rice for household use. Also, when branch families are set up, the considerations of the branch have grown far more important than those of the stem family. As the *ie* consciousness subsides, consciousness of subordinate and superior have weakened and the unique characteristic of the Japanese farm village—the familistic solidarity of the *dōzoku*—has gradually vanished.

As *dōzoku* solidarity has weakened, more intimate kinship relations formed sometimes on the basis of stem-branch relations or through affinal bonds have taken its place. These new relations are not vertically stratified as were their predecessors, with stem family at the top of the pyramid, but are horizontally formed by kinship groups which come together on an equal footing. Affinal ties, which were always inherently close, although once subordinated to stem-branch relations, are now becoming more and more important.

Affinal and stem-branch relations are different in that the latter maintain a theoretically unending relationship, while those formed through marriage begin to fade after the death of the spouses. This was particularly true with marriages between families from different villages which lacked the daily contact that makes the interaction created by affinal ties last longer. As mentioned before, the practice of exogamous marriage was almost non-existent in the rural villages of Japan, while marriages within the *dōzoku* were quite common. The farther back in history one traces middle-strata farm families, the more intrahamlet marriages are recorded. In some cases affinal relationships grew very close through daily interaction and the feelings of kinship through marriage persisted long after the death of the spouses. Even then affinal relations still did not have the permanency of stem-branch relations.

When *dōzoku* solidarity was strong, these characteristics of affinal relationships made them more personal than stem-branch relationships. All members of a house participated in the same stem-branch relation, and the son's stem family could not differ from the father's. In contrast, affinal relationships differed within the same house: the patriarch's closest affinal group was his wife's family and the heir's was his spouse's family. Within the same family, then, different members had close affinal ties with completely different families. Affinal relations created by marriage between one family and another were thus more personal than stem-branch relations. If in the course of daily affairs a man had to make an important decision, in most cases he would rely on his wife's family for advice and support. In more formal occasions which involved interaction within the village, such as weddings and funerals, however, the *dōzoku* had priority and affinal relationships were drawn into the background.

But as descent ranking in the *dōzoku* weakened, relations with brothers and uncles and affinal relations became more important than those between stem and branch. Another factor that made affinal relations more important was that when the branch family no longer looked upon its establishment as a favor bestowed by the stem family, inter-family ties began to lose their closeness. As long as the family felt that its existence was due to the benevolence of the stem, no dissatisfaction could be expressed no matter how meager the assets received. But as branch family operations became more oriented to the needs of the individual, dissatisfaction over the distribution of assets was likely to appear in either branch or stem family in cases where brothers did not get along well. In such situations, the affinal relation with the wife's parents became even closer than stem-branch relations, such as those with an older brother.

The land reform was the crucial factor which weakened the bonds of *dōzoku* group solidarity and strengthened affinal relations. Even before the war, the solidarity of branch-stem family relations was weakening in more advanced areas; sometimes the word *shinrui* (relatives), for example, was applied to all kin no matter whether they were related through the *dōzoku* or by marriage. After the war and the institution of the land reform, this trend spread uniformly throughout the country. Relations with the wife's family have grown much closer. And usually because of the greater geographical range of marriages, affinal ties are more likely to lie outside the villages, while *dōzoku* relations were almost totally confined to one village. Improvements in transportation, including widespread ownership of cars, have enabled frequent contacts with the affinal group outside the village. Shrinkage in the size or complete dissolution of cooperative labor groups organized on the basis of stem-branch relations has led to increased exchange of labor between affinal groups, particularly during the busy planting and harvesting seasons. Of course, such labor exchange is practiced only when the peak demand for labor differs because of different crops being planted or harvested. If the busiest seasons coincides for both affinal groups, greater reliance is placed on cooperation in connection with stem-branch relations. However, as already mentioned, this kind of cooperation does not take place under a stem family's leadership, but is more likely to be confined to close relatives. If interaction between siblings and between nephews and uncles, very similar to affinal interaction, becomes more important than stem-branch interaction, or if greater priority is assigned to affinal rather than *dōzoku* relations, it means that there is no difference between kinship relations on the paternal or the maternal side. This is an indication that kinship relations in the Japanese rural village are becoming more modern, which is to say pragmatic.

Stem-branch relations, however, are not totally devoid of significance. As long as the consciousness of the *ie* remains, stem-branch relations are not likely to devolve into simple kin relations nor will stem-branch ranking disappear. Kinship relations, including affinal relations, tend to restrict the freedom of the families involved. The rural family does not act without considering how those actions will affect their stem-branch or affinal relations. For example, though the wishes of the two partners in a marriage are respected and relatives are rarely consulted or their permission solicited, the family still takes into account what the relatives will think. While kinship interaction in the village occurs more frequently on the basis of the closeness of ties, duty (*giri*) is still more important than personal sentiments (*ninjō*). An adequate understanding of the importance of kinship in rural social relations is crucial to an accurate analysis of Japanese rural society.

Chapter Three
The Social Structure
of the Hamlet

Social Characteristics

The Hamlet as Community

Farmhouses in Japan usually are clustered together in hamlets which the residents most commonly call *mura*, but the word *buraku* is used as well, in order to distinguish the settlement from the larger administrative village, also designated as *mura*. Hamlets vary in configuration but are most commonly settlements of tightly clustered houses. Scattered settlements are found in mountain and foothill regions, but this pattern is exceptional. The 1970 Agricultural Census of 143,000 hamlets found that 53 percent were of the cluster type and 18 percent of the scattered mountain type. Other patterns include plain villages where fields separate one house from another (21 percent), and suburban ribbon settlements in which the houses are densely clustered along roads leading directly into a large town (8 percent).

Distribution of hamlet size is shown in Tables 18 and 19, which were compiled from two censuses and three sample surveys. Those with less than 100 households, including about 50 farming households, make up approximately 80 percent of the total. If hamlets in or adjacent to urban areas are excluded, the average size is about 70 households altogether, with slightly fewer than 40 farming households. The average number of households per hamlet varies by region, but in general the typical Japanese hamlet has no more than 50 farm households, or when both farm and non-farm households are included, no more than 100.

Table 18   Distribution of Settlements by Number of Farm Households
(percent)

Year	Number of Farm Households				
	≤9	≤29	≤49	≤99	≥100
1955	3.0	43.6	31.4	17.7	4.3
1960	2.9	44.3	30.7	17.8	4.3
1965	3.6	45.3	28.7	18.1	4.3
1970	4.2	46.2	27.4	17.0	3.9
1975	7.8	46.7	26.2	15.8	3.5

Note: Survey sample for 1955 included 20 percent of all farm villages;
for 1965, 5 percent; and for 1975, 14 percent.

Table 19   Distribution of Settlements by Total Number of Households
(percent)

Year	Number of Households				
	≤19	≤49	≤99	≤149	≥150
1960	14.0	47.0	25.3	6.9	6.7
1965	12.8	42.1	25.8	8.3	11.1
1970	15.2	41.5	24.4	8.1	10.8
1975	15.0	37.7	23.7	8.5	15.1

Japanese farmers cultivate fields that are extremely small by international standards, and about half that area is devoted to wet paddy rice. This means that almost every farm has some stake in rice production and that rice farming still constitutes a major force in the nation's agriculture. Except for a few areas of rain-fed fields, wet paddies require extensive irrigation as well as intensive labor. The members of not just one family but of many must combine their efforts and help each other in rice cultivation, and the fundamental rule of agricultural cooperation extends to many other aspects of hamlet life as well. For centuries, the *mura* or *buraku* has been a basic social unit almost as important as the *ie* for the Japanese farmer.

The construction and irrigation of wet rice paddies were possible only through the combined efforts of more than one household. An irrigation system, by nature, cannot be maintained or operated on an individual basis; the cooperative labor of the entire community was necessary. Before the use of chemical fertilizers, the mulch necessary for fertilizer was obtained in nearby forests and fields, and the hamlet controlled access to those areas so that everyone would be certain of an adequate supply. Forests were also an important source of firewood and wood for charcoal, and their management and control was another important responsibility of the entire community.

Already in the Tokugawa period, most of the farmland was owned and operated by individual households. Very few of a family's holdings, however, were contiguous; they tended to be fragmented and scattered here and there among those of other farmers. Water from the main irrigation canal did not enter each field through separate water courses, but passed through any number of fields owned by different persons, each taking his share along the way. To ensure that no one took more than his fair share of water, community control over water resources was strict. In addition, sources of timber, mulch, and charcoal—the forests and uncultivated fields—were usually owned by the hamlets rather than by individual farmers. The hamlet regulated when and in what quantity such resources could be exploited.

After the Meiji Restoration of 1868, the situation changed somewhat, and rights to private ownership of land became legally established. Community control over common resources weakened in areas where private interests began to purchase field and forest lands. But despite increased private ownership and the efforts initiated toward the end of the nineteenth century to consolidate farm fields by encouraging landowners to trade or buy more land, most farm families continued to cultivate fragmented holdings, often traveling great distances in order to tend all of their fields. Without consolidation of fields, even improvements in irrigation systems did not eliminate the need for communal control over water usage. In mountainous and foothill areas, forests and fields remained the common property of the hamlet or in some cases were registered in the name of villagers as joint owners.

Japanese villages continued to be defined as "village communities" (*Dorfgemeinde*) for many years even after World War II. As a concept the "village community" refers to one of the "forms which precede capitalistic production," a stage where the communal system characteristics of a primitive communal society are retained because low productivity makes independent farm operations impossible. In a village community, agricultural production may be predominantly an individual operation, but the farmer still requires some cooperation based on communal ownership to carry through his productive activity. Hence, the communal constraints of the closed, self-contained universe that are typical of the hamlet restrict the scope of individual activities.

Whether they are still part of contemporary communities or not, these were definitely structured characteristics of Japanese rural society until long after the Meiji Restoration. But the tenaciousness of the traditional systems should not be interpreted merely as the persistence of feudalistic forms. Rather, they persisted because Japan's capitalistic development was achieved through the exploitation of agriculture, which in turn could not be extricated from the premodern mode of production. It followed that elements of the "village community" continued to characterize Japanese hamlets throughout the period of modernization.

Since these communal characteristics persisted in agricultural production, it was only natural that the village society based on that production should continue to display equally strong communal features. The growth of the money economy in the Meiji era brought more farm families under its sway than had been the case during the Tokugawa period, but production still centered mainly on staple grains, rather than on production for the commodity market, and each household supplied almost all of its own food needs. The low level of participation in the commodities market was a major factor in preserving the more or less self-contained, autonomous nature of the hamlet and inhibiting its involvement with the outside world. In the 1920s, farmers gradually began to own bicycles, but the bicycle could not be used to travel long distances and as long as they were the only means of transportation, the hamlet remained a small universe in which the bulk of production and consumption went on independently within its boundaries. The communal nature of farm production influenced other aspects of life and assumed a lasting quality of mutual assistance in social rituals and ceremonies, marriages, funerals, or festivals, as well as of cooperation among neighbors in the construction and repair of homes and farm buildings.

Hamlet unity was symbolized by the *ujigami*, or local guardian deity. Isolation from the outside world and a sense of rivalry with neighboring villages over the right to use water and forest resources gave hamlet members a strong sense of belonging. Every moment of a villager's life was spent in close association with members of the same community, and relations with family and neighbors spanned the entire spectrum of social interaction. The individual had constantly to consider the concerns of other members of the community. The low level of mobility meant that the interrelationships among community members were not limited to any particular time, but extended back through the centuries, involving relations between families that had been going on for many generations. Such complex, multi-faceted relations weighed heavily on the individual who could not engage in any productive activity without the encumbrance of communal restraints.

The Japanese village community is said to differ from the European pattern in that its organization is distinctly vertical or hierarchical; and it is indeed heavily influenced by stratification produced by the landlord system. The farm family could survive only through the cooperative labor and assistance of its neighbors in the community, while at the same time it was held inextricably in the web of hierarchical relations formed by the landlord system. The already complex relations among relatives and neighbors, which involved intricate customs of gift-giving and labor sharing, were compounded by the heavy burden of tenant-landlord and employee-employer relations. The lower the family's status, the heavier its social restraints and the more the individuality of those at the very bottom was completely immersed in the communal order.

Many changes have occurred in these features of the hamlet in the postwar period. Land reform put an end to the conventions under which the constraints of the hamlet were a force of communal coercion closely bound to the landlord system. On the other hand, it would be a mistake to overemphasize the village community aspects of the Japanese hamlet in the decades before 1945. Historical change had already moved many big landlords into the cities. As they became more parasitic, or reduced the size of their own farming operations, small farming landlords began to substitute for the role once played in the village by the now-absent large landlords.

Although the village continued to be self-sufficient for a long time, that self-sufficiency was not total. Production of commodities gradually expanded, and the social sphere of the farm family had already begun to grow beyond the confines of the hamlet. The agricultural tasks which required communal cooperation gradually decreased, and more and more people took up jobs in areas outside the hamlet. Also, after establishment of local government in 1889, the hamlet lost its predominant position as the self-governing unit in rural Japan. In all these ways the village community character of the hamlet had been slowly transformed from long before 1945.

The dissolution of the village community was of course not uniform throughout the country, but varied by region. The greater the level of industrialization in the region, or the closer the hamlet to an urban area, the faster its communal character weakened. It remained strongest in those hamlets farthest from the cities, in the mountain regions and areas where industry was either nascent or entirely non-existent.

But, in general, the hamlet as a village community has weakened even more since the end of World War II. The communal framework of the hamlet which dictated the behavior of all villagers gradually decayed, but it did not entirely break down. The *mura* is still very much alive. Like the other important component of rural life, the *ie*, the *mura* still retains many of its traditional strengths, although somewhat diminished from its once all-powerful role. The *mura* is as yet not a vehicle of free and voluntary cooperation among independent farmers. This chapter will discuss these problems of the Japanese hamlet in greater detail below. First, a general understanding of certain realities is necessary before any structural analysis of hamlet society can be made.

The Hamlet as Agricultural Settlement

The communal character of the Japanese hamlet underwent continual change from the time of the Restoration on, a process that was accelerated by the events of the postwar period, but the hamlets described above were for the most part autonomous, independent units in the Tokugawa period. At the time of the 1970 census, Japan had 143,000 hamlets, 90 percent of which had existed prior to the Meiji Restoration, 8 percent between 1868 and 1945, and 2 percent since World War II. If Hokkaido is excluded, 135,000, or 95 percent of hamlets today, were established before 1868. As will be mentioned later, the number of administrative villages in the first year of the Meiji era was about 80,000, or 60 percent of the total, showing that settlements did not necessarily coincide with villages. However, many of these 135,000 hamlets had less than 20 households in all and were far too small to be administratively independent. Such settlements were usually subsumed as parts of larger parent villages called *oya-mura*. These exceptions notwithstanding, the typical hamlet was an independent self-governing unit during the Tokugawa period.

The boundaries of these self-governing hamlets were clearly defined, and within those boundaries the land was cultivated by members of the hamlet and by some people from other hamlets, known as *irisaku*. The hamlet was the basic unit for taxation and farmers had collective responsibility for payments. The amount of tax paid was determined according to the territorial, as opposed to personal, principle by the estimated rice yield (*kokudaka*) of all cultivated land belonging to the hamlet, including the *irisaku* plots. When a farmer cultivated land in another hamlet (*desaku*), he paid the tax out of his yield to that hamlet, not to his own. Taxes were thus paid to the feudal lord or to the shogunate by the hamlet which held the assessed land. Tokugawa-period villages were apparently very strict concerning their boundaries, and this remains true even of today's villages. The 1970 census reports that 79 percent of hamlets have clearly drawn boundaries and 83 percent have clear-cut boundaries to their cultivated fields. Considering that 10 percent were set up after 1868 and that there are always some whose boundaries are difficult to define because of geographical features, one can say that every Japanese hamlet has a clearly delineated territory. The villagers know which roads and facilities fall under the jurisdiction of their hamlet, as well as the location of *irisaku* fields.

As will be explained in greater detail in Chapter Four, some consolidation of villages had begun in the early Meiji era, but in 1889, the government began to promote a local government policy by which all hamlets would be amalgamated into larger administrative towns and villages. The size of the self-governing unit was enlarged and the villages of the Tokugawa period became part of the Meiji administrative unit of town (*machi, chō*) or village (*mura, son*), and became known at this time as *buraku*. But to the residents of the *buraku*, there was little difference between the new administrative divisions and those of the old *mura*. The general absence of autonomy on the part of the new administrative towns or villages as well as their financial limitations meant that the *buraku* remained more than a mere administrative division; in actuality it continued in its previous status as the self-governing entity. Thus, the *buraku* is the direct descendant of the Tokugawa village, and it retained the character of the agricultural settlement. The maintenance of the traditional *buraku* self-governing status even after implementation of the new local government system is one reason it remained the most important unit of rural society.

But just as the Tokugawa administrative village did not necessarily correspond to the *mura* or hamlet, the administrative *buraku* adopted during the Meiji era does not always coincide with the *buraku* as the agricultural settlement. However, the 1970 census shows that 79 percent of the settlements were also *buraku*. In only 12 percent were two or more settlements combined to form an administrative *buraku*. Nine percent were large settlements broken down into two or more smaller administrative *buraku*. This practice of dividing up large hamlets occurred mainly during the 1940s, during wartime and immediately thereafter.

In some instances, when an administrative *buraku* is made up of two or more settlements, the hamlets may share the same local deity and consolidate their communal assets and property. Most probably, hamlets of this kind were one unit during the Tokugawa period. Even small hamlets were independent self-governing units and though they sometimes worked together, it might be only in matters relating to village administration. There were opposite instances, as well, in which settlements were divided into two or more *buraku* but continued to worship the same local deity as they had done since the Tokugawa period. Many of these had remained a single entity throughout the local government amalgamation campaign of the 1890s, but were divided into two or more *buraku* during the war when rationing proved them to be too large a unit or after the war when administrative communications increased, making hamlet division necessary. In other cases the division took place before the war, and each unit became independent in self-governing functions and finances. There are other examples of hamlets which were divided into two or more administrative units, though they actually continue to maintain their unity. All of this is presented basically to illustrate the complexity of the subject and to show that the *buraku* and the settlement do not necessarily correspond.

Nevertheless, the majority of settlements, as we have seen, are *buraku* and when they have been divided it is usually only for administrative convenience. When two or more settlements were contained in one *buraku*, they were more often than not one village under the Tokugawa regime. The largest of the group was called the main or parent village and the smaller ones, branch villages. For our present purposes, the hamlet as a settlement and the *buraku* as the administrative unit may be considered one and the same.

All hamlets were agricultural production units. Even during the Tokugawa period, the hamlet was by no means totally self-sufficient in production and would often cooperate with its neighbors in building and maintaining irrigation dams and canals, or share the use of adjacent forest and fields. But most aspects of agricultural production were carried on by the hamlet itself, and each possessed its own assets and facilities, making the community united and self-sufficient.

Rivers are the major source of irrigation water for 57 percent of all hamlets today. The 1970 census also shows that 15 percent rely on reservoirs, 10 percent on mountain streams, 5 percent on spring or rain water and 3 percent on well water. Vast improvements have been made in technology for utilizing river water for irrigation, and systems have been built so that a number of villages have access to the same river source. Even in such cases, however, the hamlet is the basic unit of water control. The 1955 settlement survey shows that one-fourth of all irrigation systems at that time were contained within the confines of a single hamlet, and as many as one-third of the systems were used only by a group of farmers within the hamlet (see Table 20). A large source of water like a river naturally encompasses more than just one hamlet, but the high percentage of those using smaller irrigation sources is significant. In terms of water rights ownership, 60 percent of irrigation works are held by several hamlet members, by one hamlet, or by a group whose membership is slightly larger than one hamlet. In terms of area irrigated, works owned by groups larger than the hamlet, such as land improvement organizations or one or more municipalities, are by far the largest. Again, in all these cases the basic unit responsible for control and allocation of water to the members remains the hamlet.

Table 20 Extent and Ownership of Irrigation Systems (for prefectures excluding Hokkaido), 1955

Size	Percentage
Extends to entire administrative village or town, or to other villages and towns	15.9
Extends to adjacent settlements	24.6
Does not extend beyond the hamlet	25.5
Confined to a single or several holdings	33.6
Other	0.4
Owner	
National, prefectural, or municipal government	20.7
Land improvement district	12.8
Hamlet or private irrigation union	28.6
Joint ownership by users	29.5
Other	8.4

Hamlet ownership of forests and fields is usually considered a holdover from the communal patterns of ownership, but here too, important changes have taken place. Immediately after the Meiji Restoration, when state and private lands were divided, some hamlets relinquished their ownership of fields and forests to the government. More widespread use of commercial fertilizers meant that these areas were no longer necessary for their supplies of mulch, and many hamlets divided up ownership among member families. With the exception of Hokkaido, where conditions differ, only 47 percent of all hamlets continue to own forest and grassland. Of these more than half own the land alone, less than 30 percent own the land jointly with one or more other hamlets, while the remainder own land both jointly and independently. Eighty-two percent of these hamlets own the same land they held since before the Meiji era. Due to topographical conditions, the importance of such land varies from region to region and even within a given area, but on the whole common forest lands are not as important as they once were for the village. Nevertheless, the average holding is a generous 28 hectares, and 38 percent of farm families still hold the rights to use and benefit from these lands, an important consideration in any analysis of the rural settlement.

Over the past century, field and forest land and water use have gradually lost their previous importance as the material base of the Japanese village community. One reason is that modernization of irrigation facilities downgraded the relative weight of the individual hamlet in the irrigation system. No longer indispensable as fertilizer sources, field and forest lands have often been broken up among families in the hamlet. Propane gas is now commonly used for cooking and heating, and fuels from the forest are no longer needed. Most mountain villages no longer make their own charcoal, so commonly owned forest lands are valuable only as a source of timber production and grass fields as pastureland for cattle. Even where the common lands are still important, rationalization of management methods has greatly changed their communal character.

While control and common management of water resources have drastically changed, the peculiarities of rice production still demand a certain level of cooperation among village farmers. The 1970 census shows that only 7 percent of all hamlets do not have agricultural practice unions, and in 70 percent of settlements the unions are organized on a hamlet basis, i.e., members of the union are only members of a particular hamlet. Twenty-one percent of hamlets were too large for only one union and have two or more. Only 3 percent had organized a union in cooperation with one or more other small hamlets. The high rate of organization along hamlet lines shows clearly that the hamlet as a settlement, rather than the administrative *buraku,* is the unit of agricultural production. The level of union activity varies, some of the unions being mere transmitters of information from the local Nōkyō, or agricultural cooperative. Generally, unions now tend not to actively conduct joint projects for the farmer, another indication of the noticeable decline in hamlet-level cooperative labor. In some cases, cooperative activities involve only a few farm families. At other times, the cooperative projects involve a range of farmers broader than those within one hamlet. This is a recent trend that bears watching as an aspect of change in the farming hamlet. It is hard to draw an exact picture of change in the Japanese hamlet, but a better understanding can be reached through an examination of the results of nationwide settlement surveys.

Change in the Agricultural Settlement

The first national survey on agricultural settlements was made, though on a sample basis, as part of the 1955 National Agricultural census. The absence of nationwide statistical data from the period prior to 1945 makes comparison or contrast of prewar and postwar conditions of agricultural settlements impossible. However, 1955 marks the point at which the Japanese economy began to shift from recovery to growth, and although enormous strides were made in agriculture during the 1945–55 period, many features remained from the pre-1945 period. A comparison of farm settlement surveys made in conjunction with the World Agricultural Censuses of 1960 and 1970, and the sample surveys of 1955 and 1975, provides a fair idea of the changes that took place between the prewar and postwar periods. We can also deduce much about the conditions of subsequent change and stagnation which marked the three decades of the postwar period.

Table 21, on agricultural cooperation in *buraku* or agricultural settlements, shows that those in which application of insecticides and pesticides was a joint project had increased from 68 percent in 1955 to 84 percent in 1960. Although in 1955 only 19 percent of settlements adopted cooperative ventures for the shipping and sale of their products, 86 percent were doing so by 1960. The number of settlements with joint-use facilities also increased, and almost half had concluded agreements on wages for farm labor.

These figures suggest that the cooperative systems of the hamlet were flourishing rather than declining. In the shift from

Table 21 Distribution of Settlements by Type of Farm Cooperation (percent)

	1955	1960
Crop spraying and dusting	68	84
Packing, shipping, and sales	19	86
Use of facilities	24	42
Wage agreements	30	44
Nursery during busy season	7	12
Food preparation	0.6	0.8

self-sufficient to commodity production, any system of cooperative labor developed on the basis of self-sufficiency should gradually erode, making way for greater independence in individual farm operations. Yet the statistics seem to indicate just the opposite. Actually, however, agricultural cooperation involving the entire hamlet did not become more widespread. The reason cooperation increased among hamlet farmers in the control of insects, for example, is due less to hamlet solidarity than to other practical factors. Fewer family members, relatives, and neighbors were available to help out, and the methods of application of improved pesticides and herbicides made it next to impossible for individual farms to handle the job alone. If a helicopter were hired for crop dusting, for example, more than one village had to participate in the particular project.

Again, cooperative ventures in packing, shipping, and sales have less to do with hamlet unity than with the needs of commodity market production. Every farm in a hamlet is rarely engaged in these operations; only those farmers directly involved in the production of a given commodity crop will work together in the packing, shipping, and sales of that product. Likewise, although there are now more hamlets with cooperative facilities, such as silk cocoon hatcheries and fruit and milk depots, most, with the notable exception of community workshops, are built and maintained by the group of farmers who actually use the facilities rather than the hamlet or agricultural practice union (see Table 22). Often the construction of large-scale facilities is undertaken by the municipal government or by the local Nōkyō rather than by the *buraku* itself. Also, agreements on farm labor wages are concluded on the municipal or Nōkyō level.

With the exception of rice farming, in most crop production,

Table 22   Joint Use of Farm Facilities (percent)

	Hamlets with Joint Facility Users		Facilities Owned by Hamlet or Practice Union	
	1960	1970	1960	1970
Workshop	10.8	6.7	80.7	85.5
Crop spraying and dusting	0.4	5.3	41.6	33.2
Silkworm hatchery	7.7	17.6	18.3	37.6
Fruit		13.7	8.3	
Grading station	2.7			40.4
Vegetable		2.0	14.7	
Collecting and marketing station	11.5	18.5	49.0	69.9
Milk depot	12.0	11.3	7.9	12.0

which has grown in importance since the war, the shift from hamlet-based to broader-based organizations is readily apparent. In 1955, 47 percent of the hamlets had no farmers who belonged to organizations for specialized production, but by 1960, the proportion had dropped to 17 percent, evidence that farmers were becoming better prepared to handle commodity production (see Table 23). All types of cooperative organizations, with the exception of those for hatching silkworms, grew in number between 1955 and 1960. Most specialized cooperatives have chapters in each hamlet, which farmers within the area can join. Not every farmer belongs to these cooperatives. Obviously, a cooperative designed expressly for dairy farmers would have little to offer the farmer who has no dairy cattle. These cooperatives, however, usually include farmers from several hamlets or may be formed on the municipal or Nōkyō level. In 1955 only 19 percent of cooperatives were organized along agricultural hamlet lines, i.e. within the confines of a single hamlet. Twenty percent of cooperatives included other hamlets, 48 percent encompassed farmers throughout an entire municipality, and 13 percent were made up of members from more than one municipality. Today, cooperatives are much more likely to include members from more than one hamlet alone. Because of the decrease in population engaged in farming and the inability of agriculture to keep pace with rapid economic growth in other sectors of the economy between 1960 and 1970, cooperative unions, except for those for

Table 23   Hamlets with Participants in Specialized Cooperatives (percent)

	1955	1960	1970
Dairy	21	37	29
Poultry	10	17	16
Pigs	—	18	20
Fruit	9	20	26
Vegetable	7	18	24
Flower	2	4	6
Products for craft industries	—	28	21
Silkworm	31	30	24
Processing	3	5	3
No participants	47	17	20

fruit and truck farmers, have entered a slump or are on the decline. Nevertheless there are many more cooperative unions than before the war, and the position of the hamlet has grown much less important as the basic unit of farm production.

As pointed out above, there are two general types of farmers in Japan: the full-time farmer who produces for the commodity market and the part-time farmer who produces rice only for family consumption. Even part-time farmers may require the services of a coop which provides crop dusting, for example, while they may not need to participate in the shipping and sales cooperative. With changes such as these, the hamlet can no longer be the sole unit of farm production, but must adapt to the needs of commodity production.

Attention should also be given to the non-farm families in the hamlet. While there is no way of knowing how many hamlet families in the prewar period were not involved in farm production, the figures show that there were very few in 1955. Since the settlement survey at that time was conducted on the basis of samples, it is possible that it covered only predominantly agricultural settlements; in any case the number of non-farm households was negligible. In 1960, five years later, 39 percent of the total were non-farm households in hamlets throughout the country, and by 1970 a majority were non-farming. By 1975, the figure was 70 percent (Table 24). This large percentage is not uniform throughout the nation, however, and reflects the very

Table 24   Farm and Non-farm Households in the Agricultural Hamlet

Year	Number of Households				
	Farm Household	Full-time Farmer	Part-time Farmer Earning Most Income from Non-farm Sources	Non-farm Household	Total
1960	39	(13.4)	(12.5)	25	64
1965	38	(8.2)	(15.8)	48	86
1970	37	(5.8)	(18.8)	44	81
1975	35	(4.3)	(21.7)	83	118
	Percentage				
1960	60.9	(20.9)	(19.5)	39.1	100.0
1965	44.2	(9.5)	(18.3)	55.8	100.0
1970	45.6	(7.2)	(23.2)	54.3	100.0
1975	29.7	(3.6)	(18.3)	70.3	100.0

high percentage of non-farm families living in hamlets which have been officially designated as areas for urbanization promotion. As shown in Table 25, even in 1975, more than 40 percent of hamlets had 80 percent or more families whose livelihood was gained from farming. Still, most hamlets have more non-farm households, so that the Japanese rural village is no longer composed solely of farmers, but is described as a *konjū shakai*, or mixed society. The statistics presented in Table 24 show that full-time farmers occupy a surprisingly small minority in the hamlet. Given steady increases in the number of part-time farmers, it is now evident that the "agricultural settlement" is largely occupied by non-farm people.

A related phenomenon, shown in the 1975 settlement survey, is that 80 percent of settlements have residential land occupied by non-farm families. Of these, 4 percent had no non-farmer residential land before 1965. In 90 percent of settlements the amount of non-farm residential land has increased since 1965. Significantly, the survey also shows that 38 percent of settlements have

Table 25   Distribution of Settlements by Proportion of Farm Households (percent)

Year	≤10	≤30	≤50	≤80	≥80
1960	3.4	8.8	9.4	27.5	50.9
1975	6.8	11.4	11.0	28.5	42.2

factories employing four or more people. In 20 percent of these settlements, the factories were built between 1965 and 1975, and in 80 percent existing factory area was increased. Of course there are regional differences in the density of factory location; more than half the settlements in the heavily urbanized Kinki, Tōkai, and southern Kantō regions have factories. In sparsely populated areas of the country and areas where people leave their villages temporarily to find non-farm work, the number of villages with factories is far below the national average. Therefore, it is not valid to make the sweeping statement that since nearly 40 percent of settlements have factories, rural Japan is being overwhelmed by industrialization. The trend, however, cannot be ignored, for it represents one aspect of change in Japanese rural society.

Another important change has occurred in the type of occupations farmers gravitate toward in obtaining non-farm income. In an increasing number of families, farming is left up to the wife and older people, while the head of the house commutes to a job outside the settlement. For these househeads, the settlement home is merely a place to sleep, and such families closely resemble the non-farm families living in the hamlet. If a man cannot find work in a nearby town, he must go farther, often staying away from the farm for several months or even the greater part of the year. According to the 1970 census, 36 percent of rural villages had househeads working in distant towns, usually in a large metropolitan area, such as Tokyo or Osaka. Of all farm households in the nation, 8 percent have members working away from home. In the Tōhoku region, the proportion is much larger—one out of four. Figures show that in 80 percent of Tōhoku settlements, at least one farmer is living and working away from home. In the Tōhoku area before the war, slightly less than 30 percent of the hamlets had heads of household living and working away from home, but by 1960 the number had risen to just under 50 percent, and in 1970 to 78 percent. By way of comparison, in 3 percent of villages in the southern Kyushu region some farm families had the head of household working away from home during the prewar period; by 1960 this had increased to 16 percent, and by 1970 to 69 percent. Such a dramatic change can hardly be ignored. Although the rate at which farmers are forced to work for extended periods away from the farm has recently been slowing down, the existence of farm households where the househead must be absent for long periods is an important aspect of change in the agricultural settlement, and a phenomenon that has made the village more heterogeneous than ever before.

The hamlet is thus gradually losing its distinctiveness as a solely agricultural production community, although unity remains in other aspects of the life of rural society. Almost every settlement has either a civic hall (*kōminkan*) or meeting hall (*shūkaijō*). The 1960 census reported civic halls in 47 percent of settlements and meeting halls in 69 percent. In 1975, regular gatherings were being held at either meeting or civic halls in 68 percent of settlements. Other places of assembly include the Shintō shrines and Buddhist temples which have been in the hamlets for centuries, and although temples rarely cater to the entire population of a hamlet, they still provide important gathering places. Villagers consider the roads in the hamlet and vicinity hamlet territory, regardless of whether they are municipally owned or whether they are for farm use or for timber hauling. Repair and maintenance of the roads is commonly considered the hamlet responsibility.

Life in hamlet society has until recently been based on jointly owned assets, common-use facilities, and cooperative labor. Assets and facilities have always been thought of as belonging to the entire hamlet, and community activities have been joined by every member of the hamlet. Farmers and non-farmers, full-time and part-time and rich and poor farmers were all regarded as part of the hamlet "family." By its very nature, the agricultural practice union did include non-farm members, but the unions were an inseparable part of hamlet life. While the hamlet exerted strong restrictions on all its members, those restrictions are now loosening in the absence of an adequate material base. This is symbolized by the changes which have taken place in the ownership of common lands and in the control of irrigation facilities. One of the most important factors which loosened hamlet control and village restrictions was the abolition of the landlord system, and postwar economic and social changes have further contributed to the demise of hamlet unity. The agricultural practice union, whose express purpose is the improvement of farm production, is in most cases separate from the hamlet itself. Current realities make it impossible for the hamlet to be a self-contained, all-encompassing entity.

As we shall see below, functional groups are losing their identity with the hamlet as a whole. Traditional groups were always one and the same with the hamlet, and the same applied to the functional groups which arose in the modern era. Now, they are growing more independent, although this is a relatively recent trend. Groups closely identified with the whole hamlet still exist, and although hamlet ties are weakening, they still maintain some control over the members. Even today peace and unity are considered the supreme objectives of village life.

Social Groups in the Hamlet

Internal Organization

In the social life of the village, a farm family's closest relations are with those living in the neighborhood. These neighbors may be blood or affinal relatives, but even when not, on funeral, marriage, and festival occasions, neighbors rank next in closeness to *dōzoku* and relatives. Contact with neighbors, furthermore, is a constant and routine part of everyday life.

Relations between members of a particular neighborhood are not necessarily equally intimate; A may interact with B and C, B with A and D, C with A and E, but A have very little to do with D and E. Based on the close ties between neighbors, *kumi* (squads or groups) evolved in the hamlet, each encompassing an area broader than the immediate neighborhood. A hamlet with a very few households did not have to form *kumi*, but in larger settlements they were established for the purposes of convenience and as a basic unit of village life.

The history of the *kumi* organization dates back to the Taika Reform of 645. During the Tokugawa period, *gonin-gumi* (lit. five-man groups) were set up throughout the country to impose collective responsibility on the members. Initially established as a system of mutual surveillance to suppress Christianity, as the years went on the *gonin-gumi* also began to serve as a channel for inculcating the doctrine of frugality and hard work so that the village could meet its quota in rice tax. On occasion, the members would read the articles of association of the *gonin-gumi* and reaffirm their pledge to uphold its principles.

The Meiji government never actually institutionalized the *gonin-gumi*, and the *kumi* were not incorporated into the municipal system adopted in 1889. In small villages where *kumi* were not necessary or where *dōzoku* relations functioned in place of *kumi*, the *gonin-gumi* disappeared, but in villages where such an organization was necessary it often remained on a voluntary basis.

After the Shōwa Panic (1927), with the growth of the movement to revitalize the farm economy, attention focused on the neighborhood groups. The *kumi* were the most expedient mechanism for strengthening cooperation within the village. In 1940 neighborhood sub-groups known as *tonari-gumi* were established to ensure that everyone in the nation was informed of the decisions and actions of the national government concerning the war, and to encourage everyone to do his best in the war effort. In these organizations the *kumi* were reborn in all Japanese farm villages.

After the war, the Occupation judged the *tonari-gumi* and the neighborhood or *buraku* associations as institutions designed for the execution of war and ordered their abolition. But just as the *gonin-gumi* had continued to exist in many villages without the sanction of the Meiji government, the *tonari-gumi* continued to function even after officially abolished because they were necessary to daily life. According to the 1955 survey, only 27 percent of the villages in the country did *not* have *kumi*; such villages were small and the need for *kumi* did not arise (recall that 20 percent of hamlets at that time had 20 or fewer households). In 1955, when the *buraku* association or *tonari-gumi* system was at a low ebb after being banned by the Occupation, the *kumi* were still active in 66 percent of rural settlements.

The origins of the *tonari-gumi* can be traced back to the *gonin-gumi*, which, however, were not always organized in groups of only five households even during the Tokugawa period. Today's *kumi* usually consist of about ten households. In many large hamlets, several *kumi* form a larger group called an *ō-gumi*. The hamlet might, for example, be divided into north, east, south, and west *ō-gumi*, each made up of smaller groups, the *ko-kumi*. When the *buraku* is made up of several small, adjacent settlements, each one becomes an *ō-gumi*. The *ō-gumi* have important functions, but the *ko-gumi* are basically transmitters of information. In hamlets where there are no *ō-gumi*, the neighborhood groups function as both *ō-gumi* and *ko-gumi*, and are usually larger than the typical *ko-gumi*. Usually the *kumi* are composed of adjacent households, but geographical proximity was not always the determining factor. Sometimes the *kumi* represented a pattern of relations with the head of the *kumi* which existed prior to its organization. In still others they were formed along the genealogical lines of an *ie*. Such patterns usually ran into problems of communication and other administrative inconveniences, and most were reorganized later along geographical lines. Reorganization almost always occurred among or within the *ko-gumi*, but *ō-gumi* were rarely changed. Exceptions to this general rule occurred after the amalgamation of towns and villages in 1953 when larger administrative *buraku* were divided into units similar to *ō-gumi* to facilitate administration and communication.

Kumi were differently named according to region. In some villages the names reflect ancient traditions, as in the case of *kaito* (inside the hedges) and *kōji* (narrow street) or simply *kōchi* (cultivated land) and *tsubo* (flat land). When organized into larger *ō-gumi*, the smaller units were called *jikko-gumi* (ten-house groups), *gochō-gumi* (five-house groups), or *han* (squads). Many times the *ō-gumi* took the name of a local landmark, one of the cardinal directions, or the family name of the head. In most instances, the smaller *kumi* were numbered.

Strictly speaking, any discussion of *kumi* should deal with both *ō-gumi* and their subgroups, the *ko-gumi*, which are basically mechanisms for the relay of information, but I will limit the discussion to the *kumi* in terms of the *ō-gumi* or the *kumi* which have functioned as both *ō-gumi* or *ko-gumi*.

Kumi have many functions as subordinate units of the hamlets. In hamlet-wide, agricultural production-related activities, such as road repair or the dredging of irrigation ditches, tasks are assigned to each *kumi*. The *kumi* commonly correspond to units of the agricultural practice union. It was common for tasks in rice planting to be allocated on a *kumi* basis. Except for villages where *dōzoku* groups formed organizations for farm work, the *kumi* was the unit of cooperative labor in agricultural production. Throughout the centuries, when productivity was low, the *kumi* had proportionately increased importance.

In the non-agricultural aspects of life in the village, the *kumi* have been organizations of mutual assistance to help villagers at marriages and births, and at times of natural disaster or other misfortune. Often *kumi* served as the funeral *kumi* which helped out members on the death of family members. Another example of the *kumi* role in providing for the needs of ceremonial occasions was that it often owned the eating utensils and furnishings required by the rules of etiquette. Also, when thatched roofs were still a common sight in the Japanese countryside, it was often the *kumi* which cooperated to provide labor for renewing them. In some villages, the *kumi* would cut straw from commonly owned fields and thatch the roofs for each household in turn.

The *kumi* functioned as organizations subordinate to the *ujiko* group, the group made up of persons under the protection of a village deity. In general, all residents of the village were *ujiko* of equal status, but in some cases they were not, sometimes giving rise to complex problems, as will be discussed later. In larger villages, each *kumi* took turns handling the affairs of festivals and ceremonies held in celebration of the deity. In certain other religious rites, such as Buddhist *kōshin-kō* and *himachi-kō* when all villagers were to participate, since it was impossible for everyone to join in the preparations, the *ō-gumi* would usually take turns in organizing the occasion.

In the past the *kumi* played a part in almost every aspect of village life, but its role has declined with the increase in agricultural productivity and the concomitant expansion of independent operations. In aspects of agriculture in which *kumi* are still active today, the most important is in the maintenance of roads and irrigation ditches. In rice planting and other tasks, the sphere of cooperation has shrunk considerably and only relatives and close neighbors are relied on for help. The *kumi* no longer need supply cups, bowls, and other utensils for ceremonial occasions since the higher standard of living has made it possible for most families to maintain their own supplies. The thatched roof has become conspicuous by its rarity, having been in most cases replaced by tile or sheet metal, so that the *kumi* function of mending and replacing thatch roofs, too, has been virtually eliminated.

Though various traditional groups with special functions were organized which included the same members as the *kumi*, in many instances they encompassed two or more *kumi*. As will be discussed in the following section, these special functions were not identified with those of the *kumi*, and with the passage of time, the importance of the special groups faded. Even when functional groups created since the early Meiji era had exactly the same membership as the *kumi*, they did not necessarily strengthen the functions of the *kumi*. Although the groups making up the agricultural practice unions were identical in membership composition to the *kumi*, the presence of non-farming households which did not belong to the unions meant that the *kumi* and the union remained distinct.

Just as the hamlet has become a separate organization from the functional associations to which its members belong, the *kumi* are no longer traditional groups overlapping in membership with sub-units of various groups but have handed their duties over to the functional associations, becoming little more than units of geographical convenience in the hamlet. Like the small neighborhood groups, the *kumi* are likely to be relegated to the position of information transmission vehicles for the hamlet, which has itself become essentially the lowest echelon in local government.

Nevertheless, the hamlet still retains some undifferentiated functions, and the *kumi* have not been totally changed into units of geographical convenience or simply for transmitting information. Although the *kumi* are not as important today, and do not retain their past status, they are still essential elements of the internal structure of the hamlet.

Traditional Hamlet Groups

In the past, the hamlet functioned smoothly as one unit, and the *kumi* were sub-sectors of that unit. Yet sometime during the Tokugawa period several different types of social organizations appeared in the hamlet and took their place alongside the *kumi*. Such groups were identified by their special function or task, but even then they were not differentiated from the hamlet, and their membership was identical to that of the hamlet, their activities part of village activities. The *kumi* itself performed a variety of functions, at times playing the role of a special group. Certain groups, however, did not automatically include all hamlet or *kumi* members, but admitted only those with special qualifications, or those capable of carrying out the particular group objectives. These groups, however, should not be confused with the modern functional associations, for their principles of organization were different from the voluntarism of the latter. One distinctive feature of these organizations was that possession of the qualifications for membership automatically made one a member, even if he was not especially interested either in membership or the aims of the group. These groups, which have been in existence since before the end of the Tokugawa period, will be called traditional social groups for the purposes of this study.

The first type of traditional social group to be discussed is that formed on the basis of age, rather than in terms of geography, as with the horizontally organized *kumi*. It should be understood, however, that not every village in Japan had groups organized on the basis of age, nor was there a strict requirement throughout the country for membership in some peer groups, for in some instances the members of certain households were exempted from membership in age-determined groups. The membership rules of youth groups might, for example, exempt the eldest son of the local *oyakata* or exclude persons whose parents were not natives of the village. In some villages, there might be two peer groups of exactly the same function, one for the upper class, the other for middle and lower classes. Age-level divisions varied from region to region, but almost every village had an organization for young people, although in the prewar period very few had any for small children or elderly people. Broadly speaking, age-based groups were for older children, for young people, and for middle-aged and elderly people.

Groups for children had such names as *kowakaren* and *tenjinkō*, but they were only formed on an ad hoc basis when some special occasion required, such as for a local Shintō festival. Only in exceptional cases were children's groups well defined in organization. After the war, children's organizations gradually increased in number, and the census reported in 1975 that 77 percent of all settlements had some such association. These groups usually held their meetings in private homes or in civic halls. The patterns of organization of children's groups show clear signs of change after the war and a general increase in numbers.

Groups of young men were traditionally known as *wakamono-gumi* or *wakashū-gumi*, and were and still are the most common age group in rural society. Members were ranked according to age and date of entrance into the group; and even in the case of young men adopted by marriage into hamlet families, though older, they were ranked with other newly initiated members. Centered around its leader (the *wakamono-gashira*), the group participated in various hamlet activities, such as auxiliary police functions, cooperative labor projects, and the management of local shrine festivals and rites. In farming-fishing villages, it was common for the youth to gather for several nights of socializing and training of various types at a kind of clubhouse known as the *wakamono-yado*. The role of the *wakamono-gumi* was undifferentiated until the modern era when separate volunteer fire brigades (*shō-bō-dan*) and youth corps (*seinen-dan*) were formed. Although the groups were called *wakamono-gumi*, meaning literally a corps of young men in their teens and twenties, most stayed on until well into early middle age. In hamlets where common field and forest lands remained important, the role of the *wakamono-gumi* in managing and tending such lands meant that they continued to function independently of the *seinen-dan*.

Moving up the age ladder, we come to the *chūrō-gumi*, the group of people who were too old for the youth groups, usually in their 40s and 50s; but this type of group was not particularly common. When such groups did exist, they seldom were *kumi*-type groups, and their main function was to serve as advisors to the younger groups. During the 1930s, as the country mobilized for war, groups of middle-aged people known as *sōnen-dan* were organized to further the war effort. The principal membership of the fire brigades was almost always drawn from this age group.

At the top of the hierarchy were the senior citizens, but they were seldom organized into formal age groups. More commonly, those who were over 61 and retired took part in one of the religious *kō* associations. Today, older people are more often organized in senior citizens' clubs (*rōjin kurabu*), and the 1975 census showed that they exist in some form in 84 percent of all rural settlements, a figure probably equivalent to the number of villages with active senior citizens. Meeting places of the clubs for the elderly are municipal public halls (for 25 percent of villages) and civic halls (for 53 percent), while others meet at local temples or shrines.

The second type of traditional organization is the funeral *kumi*, and this is identical in membership to the neighborhood *kumi*. Unlike other rites and ceremonies in the village, funerals cannot be scheduled, and cooperation between neighbors is particularly in need upon the death of some person in the village. In villages with strong *dōzoku* unity, the stem and branch families would be the chief functionaries for the funeral and little help would be required from one's neighbors, or from the funeral *kumi*. Funeral *kumi* were also not required in areas where one special group of families traditionally prepared the body for burial, and assistance was provided by the regular neighborhood *kumi*. Funeral *kumi* were very necessary in the small settlements where the entire hamlet would join in to help. But even in settlements without a special organization, ways were devised so that funerals would be taken care of by the group, and many of these methods were similar to the funeral *kumi*. According to the 1955 farm settlement survey, 94 percent of hamlets had some type of association for handling funerals, although its form varied. In many settlements, the *ō-gumi* would function as the funeral *kumi*; in others, two or three ordinary *kumi* would band together to perform such services. Sometimes funeral *kumi* were formed as totally separate organizations from other *kumi*. In any case, some kind of *kumi* helped in preparations and arrangements for funerals. When a person died, all the other members of the *kumi* would bring a fixed amount of rice and cash to the bereaved family and take over all funeral arrangements including informing of relatives, notifying the local Buddhist temple, preparing equipment for the funeral, digging the grave, performing pallbearer duties, and serving food to the mourners. It was common in most villages for lunch to be served right before the deceased was taken to the cemetery, and the meal would be prepared by the *kumi* housewives. It was also customary to decide who would travel to inform relatives far away of the death, who would serve as pall-bearers, and who would dig the grave, all on the basis of *kumi* membership. As transportation and communication have improved, these tasks are left more and more to the local under-taker, and the responsibilities of the funeral *kumi* have greatly diminished.

Another group essential to village life was the *ujiko shūdan*, or religious group of those protected by the local deity. A distinctive feature of the Shintō pantheon is that the *ujigami* (lit., clan deity) is also the guardian god of the village. In ancient Japan, *dōzoku* group members, or *ujibito*, worshiped this deity as the guardian of their clan. As the centuries progressed and *dōzoku* subordinates established households of their own, they, too, took part in the rites celebrating the clan deity. Hence, the *ujigami* became the main deity for the entire village. But regional traditions and village structure did not always assure that all *ujiko* were accorded equal status within the *ujiko* group, and in some instances, not all members of the village were allowed to become members of the *ujiko* group. It was common for the original *honke*, the stem family that had established the village centuries before, to occupy a special position of privilege in the village, that of keeper of the shrine keys (*kagimoto*), by virtue of the fact that their family deity had become the deity of the entire village. Another system retained for a long time in some areas was that of the *miyaza*. *Miyaza* groups were made up of certain families with qualifications of lineage which gave them special duties in the supervision and conduct of ritual affairs, and each *miyaza* took its turn in handling those rituals. The family which led the *miyaza* was known as the *tōya*. The entire *ujiko* group was hierarchically stratified, but with the passage of time, it became largely symbolic and greatly simplified in function. If entrance to the *ujiko* group were restricted as in ancient times, it would differ from basic hamlet organization, but since restrictions on membership were dropped after the war, there is no longer any difference between the *ujiko* group and the hamlet. According to a preliminary survey to the 1970 census, 63 percent of all settlements have their own *ujigami*, 27 percent celebrate an *ujigami* in conjunction with one or more other hamlets, and 10 percent have no *ujigami*. These statistics show that an *ujiko* group is not always identical with the hamlet group, but that people in hamlets with an *ujigami* pay homage to one local god. There are still examples of *ujiko-sōdai* (representatives) who come from families with traditionally high status, but this does not mean that the *ujiko* group still retains its status and class orientation. One practice that generally remains is for different *kumi* to take turns in handling the affairs of festivals in honor of the *ujigami*.

Another religious group is the *kō*. *Kō* originally meant a lecture on the Buddhist sutras but was gradually broadened to refer to the group that came to listen to those lectures. Regional differences have produced many different types of *kō*, so that it is difficult to generalize, but they are roughly divisible into three types, in terms of organization: those which correspond in framework to the hamlet or the *ō-gumi*, those whose main purpose was to pool funds for activities, such as pilgrimages to Buddhist temples or Shintō shrines, and those formed on the basis of age or sex.

Examples of the first type are the *yama-no-kami* (mountain gods), *ta-no-kami* (paddy gods), *kōshin* (night vigil service), *himachi* ("waiting for the rising sun"), and the *daishi* ("great teacher Kōbō") associations. Refreshments were usually served at *kō* meetings, and members always brought along rice or cash for that purpose. Another type of *kō* with branches throughout the nation, seen in hamlets with many followers of True Pure Land Buddhism, is the *hōon-kō*, formed expressly for the purpose of conducting memorial services for the sect's founder, Shinran, on the anniversary of his death.

Examples of the second type are those whose names have been taken from famous temples or shrines, such as the Ise-*kō*, the Kompira-*kō*, and the Akiba-*kō*. Members are sent to attend rites at head shrines or temples, the Grand Shrine at Ise, the Kompira shrine in Kagawa Prefecture, the Akiba shrine and Akiba temple in Shizuoka, and also periodically gather for fellowship at members' homes to celebrate and enjoy good food and drink. Unlike the first type of *kō* in which everyone in the village participates, these *kō* are usually made up of members from only certain households. Members must naturally have the financial resources to enable them to make contributions and bear the cost of pilgrimages.

Among the last group, those for children were so insignificant in number that they hardly warrant mention. But those for women, including the *koyasu-kō*, which were formed to pray for safe childbirth, and the Kannon-*kō*, in honor of the bodhisattva of mercy, are important because they were two of the very few occasions for recreation for the young married women of the village, an opportunity to escape the pressures and hardships of their lives. One type of *kō* for elderly people was the *Nembutsu-kō*, its name taken from the chant "Namu Amida Butsu" (Hail to the Compassionate Buddha). The *Nembutsu-kō* held regular meetings at the village temple, with refreshments and conversation, and if there was a funeral in the village, the group would chant sutras for the deceased. As previously mentioned, many of these groups have now been reorganized as senior citizens' groups.

In recent years, the *kō* organizations have become more recreational than religious, and with many other alternatives for recreation available to the farm family, many *kō* have ceased to exist. Another reason for the disappearance of the prewar *kō* was that with the material shortages of wartime, the food and drink so essential to the good cheer provided at these meetings became scarce and the *kō* canceled more and more of their meetings until they were finally forced into permanent suspension. Despite the decline, however, the 1955 settlement survey shows that only 35 percent of the hamlets did not have a religious *kō*, while 43 percent had one to two, 17 percent three or four, and 5 percent five or more such organizations. Since then, many have gone out of existence, and in those that remain, the functions are much more simplified than during prewar times.

In connection with the religious *kō*, mention should be made of the *tanomoshi-kō* and the *mujin*, both kinds of mutual savings and loan associations. The *tanomoshi-kō* were originally subsidiaries of the religious *kō*, but later the direct relationship was ended and they continued with the same functions as the non-sectarian *mujin*. Today both the *tanomoshi-kō* and the *mujin* are relics of the past. Some villages had organized *fuki* (thatch) *mujin* to help families finance the rethatching of their main house or other buildings. There were also *uma* (horse) *mujin* for making loans to purchase draft animals, and *futon-mujin* for buying new furniture and bedding. Almost none of these exist today. The 1955 hamlet survey found *tanomoshi-kō* and *mujin* of many years' standing in only 12 percent of all hamlets. New *mujin* had been established for the purchase of sewing machines in 13 percent of the settlements surveyed, but by now almost all such mutual savings and loan associations have disappeared.

The last of the traditional organizations to be discussed here are the "parishioners" groups. When the Tokugawa shogunate proscribed Christianity in the seventeenth centry, it required that every person in the nation be registered at a Buddhist temple. Since many hamlets did not have their own temple, families often registered as parishioners (*danka*) of temples elsewhere with which they had had some previous connection. Even if the hamlet had a temple, they might register elsewhere because of some historical bond. Except when all hamlet people were members of the same Buddhist sect and all were registered at the same temple, the residents of the hamlet and the members of the parishioner groups were not equivalent. Though all hamlet residents worshiped the same Shintō *ujigami*, and all belonged to the same *ujiko* group, different families might be members of different Buddhist temples. However, a relatively large number of families in any one village might be registered at the same temple, and when it was a village temple, it was often an important factor in village life. Even the families which did not belong to the parishioner group of the majority participated in the rites of the local temple, and they were often connected as a worshiper group even though the sect of the village temple and their temple of registry were not the same.

Except for a few special cases, the traditional social groups were an intrinsic part of hamlet and *kumi*. In most, membership was not open to all. The *kō* which collected money for pilgrimages by members had relatively high voluntary participation, but once the organization was well established, membership was fixed, and it became difficult to drop out of a *kō*. In theory, families were free to select their own temple, but the tradition of ancestor worship did not permit the *ie* entirely free choice.

With Japan's entrance into the modern period, many of these groups began to lose their original functions. The *wakamono-gumi*, the most pervasive, was generally absorbed into the new *seinendan* which were promoted by the central government. In some hamlets the *wakamono-gumi* continued to exist and to perform special tasks in the management of hamlet-owned fields and forests, and in certain religious rites and seasonal festivals. In most cases, their original duties were taken over by the *seinen-dan*. The funeral *kumi* still performs some functions, but the scope of cooperation has greatly diminished. The *ujiko* group is now more egalitarian, and the elitism of the past is almost imperceptible. The families that once monopolized the lead roles in festivals and ceremonies can no longer handle the financial burden that these impose because of the lowering of their economic position since the land reform (1947–50). In addition, the influence of democracy on hamlet people is such that the kind of class distinctions which were once implicit on religious occasions will not be tolerated. The religious *kō* have lost their prominence as well. Fading religious fervor is part of the reason, but more importantly, the opportunity for recreation they offered has now been replaced by various other entertainments. *Kō* for women, as well, have been replaced by women's clubs and the women's division of Nō-kyō.

With the exception of traditional hamlet groups which still perform certain necessary functions, most have become history or have been almost completely transformed. Those that remain are supported by tradition and custom, but are less necessary now than in the prewar period. They nevertheless remain an important aspect of the background of rural life. Festivals for the guardian deity are still major events, and groups which work together for funerals still have an important influence on people's conduct in the village. An important route of communication is still alive in the exchanges that take place over food and drink at the *kō*.

Functional Associations and the Hamlet

The first system of local government was set up in 1889, and under it smaller hamlets were amalgamated into towns or villages. From then on each of the smaller hamlets was called a *buraku*. At the turn of the century, many different types of groups were formed under central government direction and the administrative town or village became the basic unit of their organization, with branches and subdivisions set up in each of the *buraku*.

Chief among these new groups based on age or sex were the *seinen-dan*, the women's associations (*fujinkai*), and the young women's groups (*joshi seinen-dan*) or the maidens' associations (*shojokai*), as well as those for maintaining law and order such as the "volunteer" fire brigades (*shōbō-gumi*) or security guards brigade (*keibō-dan*). In addition, in 1910 the Imperial Reservists' Association was established with local chapters composed of former servicemen and those who had not yet served in the military but had passed the physical examination for conscription. All of these were functional groups and many of them supplanted the traditional groups in form and operation.

However, membership in these organizations was obligatory. They were government-sponsored groups established in each administrative village and town, and their hamlet branches were buttressed by the high level of communal solidarity which already existed. No one could join or drop out as he or she desired, and even though membership was formally optional, in actuality qualified persons could be forced to join. For example, all men from the age of 14 to 25 and in some communities to 42 were required to be members of the *seinen-dan*, and at least 1 woman from each household had to belong to the women's association· Membership in the "volunteer" fire brigade was obligatory as well. The hamlet was thus the basis of organization for all of these groups.

The organizational nature of these groups reveals the strength of hamlet solidarity as well as the high degree of central government control that permeated every part of the nation even on the local level. The nature of agricultural groups was such that they were always easily manipulated by government authority which could create and use rural groups for its own ends. Since these organizations were formed so that every hamlet family took part, the people soon began to think of the new organizations as part and parcel of the hamlet, just as they did with traditional organizations. There was no feeling that these organizations had been foisted upon them from without, and the villagers felt it their natural duty to pay for the *seinen-dan*, the women's association, and the volunteer fire brigade from the meager funds in their village treasury. Since the organizations were thought of as intertwined with, rather than independent of, the hamlet, their growth had the "feed-back" effect of fostering hamlet unity. The fire brigade's duties included not only preventing and fighting fires and controlling floods, but some police functions as well, just as with the former *wakamono-gumi*. The functions of the *wakamono-gumi* were thus increasingly supplanted by the fire brigades and the *seinen-dan*.

The organizational characteristics of the hamlet were also apparent in the local farm unions (*nōka kogumiai*), predecessors of the present agricultural practice unions, that sprang up throughout the country after the Shōwa Panic of 1927. One of their functions was to reinforce the industrial cooperatives, which were organized for the first time in the years before World War I in the wake of the 1900 Industrial Cooperative Act. By the end of the 1920s, industrial coops were in operation in every part of the nation, and most of them coincided territorially with the boundaries of the administrative village or town. Functioning partly as a sub-unit of the village industrial cooperative, at least one local farm union was organized in each hamlet. In some hamlets, the unions were divided into even smaller units, but in those instances, it was the general rule that the *kumi* was the basis for each unit. Under such an organizational set-up, each family was forced to participate, whether it wanted to or not, another example of induced hamlet solidarity. From the standpoint of the government, the local farm union was a device to unify the farmers on the basis of communal control. It was expected to inculcate diligence and thrift, thereby acting as a main force in the rural reconstruction movement of the early Shōwa era.

Only farm families could be union members, but in almost every hamlet the union was identified with the hamlet as a whole. In many cases, it was the hamlet authority which collected dues from the villagers, as in the case of the *suiri kumiai*, or water rights unions. With technological advances in irrigation control and systems, water rights unions were organized in many areas, but membership was usually limited to landowners. Membership fees were collected from landlords, owner-farmers, and part-owners, while tenants could not become members. Nevertheless, union membership fees were collected by the *buraku* along with hamlet dues.

Almost all functional groups before the war were inseparable from the hamlet. One exception was the farmers' unions (*nōmin kumiai*) which began to spread to various parts of the country around 1920. These unions were made up of tenant and part-tenant farmers who had joined together to pressure landlords into reducing or suspending rents, and on this point they are essentially different from any of the other organizations in which all farmers participated. But the paternalistic character of relations between tenant and landlord prevented many tenants from joining, so that it was seldom that every tenant farmer in a hamlet belonged to a farmers' union. In villages under the strong control of the landlord system, it was next to impossible to organize a tenant farmers' union not consonant with the principle of hamlet holism. On the other hand, in regions where extensive lands were held by powerful landlords and all farmers tended to be tenants, the unions were often able to force the entire hamlet to join the union by effectively ostracizing the landlords' agents. Even in class-oriented interest groups like the farmers' unions, the principle of hamlet holism was all-important.

At their height, the farmers' unions never listed more than 5,000 local branches, embracing 300,000 members. In 1935, the unions were involved in almost 7,000 tenancy disputes, which suggests a fairly widespread movement, despite the fact that unions were not active in all villages in the nation (see Table 26). As the country mobilized for war, an increasingly militaristic government ordered the suppression of the farmers' unions, forcing them to disband or cease all activities. The central government sought to replace the dynamics of the union movement with new goals, forging tighter hamlet unity and reorienting it under the slogan "Construction of Villages for the Empire." The labor shortage resulting from the prosecution of war beginning in 1937 made it necessary that cooperative labor be augmented on

Table 26   Farmers' Unions and Tenancy Disputes

Year	Farmers' Unions	Union Members	Disputes	Participants in Disputes
1925	3,496	307,000	2,208	125,000
1930	4,208	301,000	2,478	59,000
1935	4,011	242,000	6,824	113,000

the hamlet and the *kumi* level. In order to sustain the supply of staple foods for the nation, the government reinforced the instruments of social control already existing in the hamlet.

This situation changed drastically during the Occupation. When the land reform was initiated, landlords tried to repossess their farm holdings. Many farmers' unions were organized to counter landlord efforts to thwart the reform. The formation of unions produced considerable unrest as the tension and conflict of a class struggle proved threatening to the principle of hamlet holism. Under orders from Occupation forces, however, the government enforced a rapid dissolution of landlord holdings, and social tensions in the villages were diffused before they developed into large-scale conflict. After the completion of the land reform, the farmers' unions either disbanded or became totally inactive. But a concomitant weakening of the social cohesiveness of the hamlet had already taken place.

Upon completion of the land reform, voluntary associations known as agricultural study groups sprang up throughout the nation. The hamlet study groups were generally composed of younger farmers who wanted to learn more about farm technology, how to raise productivity and increase the income of their farms. Usually these men were the househeads or heirs to a full-time farm household, and the organization of these study groups was distinct from the hamlet itself. Study groups were not organized everywhere, and the 1955 survey shows that at their height, only 31 percent of rural villages had such groups. Yet these study groups had an importance far beyond their number, for they marked the formation of a new organization in the rural village. If they had been organized in the pre-1945 period, they would have become part of the hamlet's formal organization and participation would have been compulsory. By 1960, study groups existed in about 30 percent of the hamlets, a slight decrease attributable in part to the decline in study of rice cultivation techniques and in part to the shift from research to applied projects for joint purchase and sales. Another important factor in this decline was that by 1960 there were fewer younger men in the hamlet to participate, and by 1975 the number of study groups still functioning was negligible.

As production of agricultural commodities, such as fruit, dairy products, poultry, livestock, and silk cocoons, grew more active after the war, many more cooperatives and organizations for joint packing, shipping, and sales were created. They are usually composed only of those farmers engaged in a particular type of production. A large membership is advantageous to such groups, so their organizational framework usually extends far beyond the hamlet, encompassing an entire administrative village. Except for associations where the majority of hamlet farmers are members, most cooperatives have no direct relation to the hamlet as a whole. During the prewar period, the union of silk cocoon raisers and the fruit growers' cooperatives were much larger than the hamlet, but the subsections of those were congruent with the hamlet and inseparable from it. The postwar cooperatives retain some features of hamlet holism, but they are far more independent of the hamlet than formerly.

Since 1955, new organizations have appeared, one express purpose of which is to facilitate cooperative farm operation or management. When farmers are all engaged in producing the same kind of fruit, for example, the cooperatives reflect traditional patterns of hamlet solidarity, but the new organizations are composed of only a few hamlet farmers and are thus distinct from established hamlet institutions. The new cooperatives range in type from cooperative labor to joint management groups. But few of these resemble the traditional patterns of cooperation. In fact, their deviation from tradition has been an element of weakness in these cooperatives, and many have subsequently been disbanded. New cooperatives were being formed at a faster rate than they were disappearing until 1966 when there were more than 6,000. After that time, the number dissolved was greater, and by 1975 there were only 4,000 new cooperatives throughout the nation. Less because of external factors, such as price fluctuations, the demise of the new cooperatives was caused in large part by the inability of members to get along well, dissatisfaction with group management, and lack of incentive in joint operations. Although the scope of cooperative operations is small, each consisting of only a few households, internal factors have often caused such efforts to fail. For farmers familiar only with hamlet-centered cooperation which suppressed individual interest in favor of devotion to the whole community, the new cooperative ventures are a real novelty. The contemporary farmer still tends to believe that all community members without exception should cooperate in group efforts.

Despite the lack of an overall increase in joint management and cooperative operations, a move was made to incorporate agricultural practice unions in 1962 through partial revision of the Agricultural Land Act and the Agricultural Cooperative Associations Law. In 1966 about 20 percent of all cooperatives were incorporated, and by 1975 the proportion had risen to almost 70 percent (see Table 27). Some cooperatives are run as joint stock companies, and although their numbers are still small, this is an important trend. These developments will contribute to greater rationalization and stability of cooperative ventures and if this trend becomes widespread, Japanese rural organization could enter a whole new phase.

Table 27 Agricultural Production Cooperatives

	1965	1970	1975
Total	5,884	4,696	4,164
Incorporated agricultural practice union	846	2,042	2,864
Cooperatives run as joint stock companies	—	522	689

About 40 percent of incorporated production cooperatives are composed of livestock farmers, less than 20 percent of fruit-growers, and just more than 10 percent of rice-paddy cultivators. Significantly, wet-rice growers began to engage in joint cultivation around 1960, a trend which has kept pace with the increase in part-time farming. Joint rice cultivation groups are of two types: one for joint use of farm machines and facilities; and the other for collective cultivation based on agreements relating to cultivation alone or to shared use of farm machinery and facilities. The latter type of organization is on the decline, but joint users' groups have more than doubled in the past several years (see Table 28).

Table 28 Rice Production Groups

	1968	1972	1976
Joint users' groups	4,257	5,093	8,964
Joint cultivation groups	6,353	5,354	3,371

Trust organizations, too, are on the increase, groups in which member farmers farm all or part of someone else's land and are paid a certain fee. About half such organizations now operating are local Nōkyō, a type of arrangement which will undoubtedly become more popular in the future. However, hamlets where rice farmers are allied in the joint-user or cultivation groups are still a very small minority; only 15 percent were organizations formed by the entire hamlet, for rice farming tends to encourage communal control. The vast increase in the number of part-time farmers has meant that cooperative organizations are maintained only through the sacrifices of a few full-time farmers. In view of this heavy burden of the full-time farmer, responsibility for organizational management is shifting away from the hamlet to voluntary associations, as reflected in the figures shown in Table 29. Although on the increase, such voluntary organizations are still very few in number throughout the nation. There is still a long way to go before full-time farmers, finally liberated from the fetters of hamlet control, can develop agriculture as a rational enterprise in the spirit of cooperation among themselves.

The vestiges of traditional organizational patterns are visible in other groups as well. The *seinen-dan* were reorganized after the war so that women could also become members, and membership is no longer compulsory. Housewives' associations and "brides' study groups" (*wakazuma gakkyū*) became voluntary. Yet in each case the idea persists that membership is obligatory. Lacking the sense of voluntary participation, many of these groups tend to sink into inactivity. Many *seinen-dan* find it almost impossible to continue because a large number of young men

Table 29 Rice Production Groups by Management (percent)

	Municipal, Nōkyō, or Other	Agricultural Practice Union	Farm Settlement	Voluntary Union or Association	Special Group
Group Cultivation					
1972	0.5	0.5	44.7	39.4	14.8
1976	0.4	2.1	29.1	54.0	14.3
Joint Use					
1972	1.2	1.0	19.6	62.9	15.3
1976	0.7	0.5	15.8	73.5	9.6

commute to non-farm jobs or have left the hamlet completely; housewives' associations are similarly inactive. To ameliorate the situation, Nōkyō has formed its own women's and youth divisions, and since members of these organizations are drawn from within the coop's local district, they are another instance of groups organized beyond the confines of the hamlet, but their sub-units are usually formed on a hamlet basis. Hamlet holism is still an effective principle of organization.

The same principle underlies the agricultural practice unions set up in prewar times. The compulsory communal labor groups organized to compensate for wartime labor shortages were, of course, disbanded after the war, but the practice unions continue, usually as subsidiaries to Nōkyō. Subsequent progress in agricultural production required that the practice unions develop new forms of cooperation, as in the use of herbicides and pesticides. Given current agricultural technology, it is much more economical for pesticides and insecticides to be broadcast large-scale, and it is imperative that all farmers in the hamlet share the expenses as well as the benefits of crop-dusting projects. Although even today the union is still identified with the hamlet itself, different levels of participation by full-time farmers, part-time farmers, and non-farmers, as well as differences in the needs and requirements of each of these groups, have made it difficult for the entire hamlet to function as a single unit. Distinction between hamlet and functional organizations seems more and more inevitable. In short, groups are now beginning to function only for the specific objectives for which they were created. To some extent, the split between the microcosmic society of the hamlet and functional groups is visible everywhere and may eventually lead to the creation of a new type of hamlet.

Institutions of Hamlet Self-Government and Their Operations

Institutions

During the Tokugawa period, the village or *mura* was administered by three leaders, the *jikata-san'yaku*. These consisted of the village head, known as the *nanushi, shōya, kimoiri,* or other names which varied from area to area; the *kumi* chiefs (*kumigashira*); and the farmers' representatives (*hyakushōdai*). Every village had its rules and by-laws, written or unwritten and sanctioned by the village assembly. Violators of those rules were punished by the hamlet. Although subject to control by the feudal lord, the hamlet was largely responsible for its legislative, administrative, and judicial affairs. After the beginning of the Meiji era and the institution of the local government system in 1889, the self-governing hamlets were combined to form administrative villages, but they were not legally recognized as independent corporate entities.

Although officially incorporated into the new administrative villages, the old *mura* continued their self-governing functions. The administrative village was not powerful enough to take over all the governing functions of the *mura,* and they remained an indispensable locus of self-government. Article 68 of the 1889 Local Government Law stipulated that "for administrative convenience, subdivisions will be created and a district chief and one deputy appointed." In most cases, these subdivisions were the old *mura.* For administrative purposes, it was easier to use the existing hamlets which had been the previous unit of self-government than to create totally new units.

Thus the hamlets, now known as *buraku,* took on a dual character, combining their self-governing role with the new function as village administration sub-unit. Hamlets owning rather large expanses of field and forest were allowed to form "property corporations" (*zaisanku*) to manage that land, an additional role which further complicated the hamlet organization. There was not always an exact correspondence between *buraku,* administrative district, property corporation, and traditional hamlet. While they were basically all distinct in character, they usually overlapped in membership. For the purposes of this discussion, I shall call the *buraku* which functioned as the administrative unit the hamlet, and the *buraku's* self-governing activities hamlet self-government.

It must also be kept in mind that a member of the administrative hamlet was not necessarily a member of the traditional self-governing community. The members of the administrative hamlet included every individual living within a prescribed geographical area. But while the hamlet included all the residents of a certain area as a self-governing social unit, it did not give equal status to everyone. Generally speaking the only households which were recognized participants in hamlet self-government were those who had lived in the hamlet for a certain period of time, paid dues to the hamlet administration, performed their share of community labor, and followed the traditional patterns of participation in funerals, festivals, gift exchange, and other customs. A family which moved in from another village could be a member only after such conditions of membership had been met, and until then it was considered merely transient. In hamlets where communal property was an overriding concern, a family could not be a full-fledged member of the community until it had purchased shares in that property. The 1955 settlement survey examined the qualifications necessary to hold rights in common land and, as Table 30 shows, residence in the hamlet alone was the condition in less than a quarter of all settlements, indicating that there were considerable differences in the rights and obligations among residents.

Table 30   Conditions for Holding Rights to Common Lands, 1955 (percent)

	New Entrant	Branch Family
Purchase of share	7.1	6.6
Decision of governing body and admission fee	13.6	11.5
Decision of governing body only	16.7	17.0
Membership fee only	7.3	6.4
Must be farmer	1.9	2.3
Minimum period of residence	11.3	9.4
Residence in the hamlet	24.6	21.4
No precedent	15.8	23.8

Nevertheless, it was not particularly difficult to become a hamlet member, and relatively few hamlets today make share-owning a requirement for membership, a change corresponding to the transformations in the structure of modern rural society. This subject is an important one and will be taken up more thoroughly later.

Let us now examine the structure of hamlet self-government. At the top of the organizational structure of government in the hamlet was the headman. During the Meiji era, the hamlet head was also known as the *sōdai*, but after the establishment of the local government system in 1889, the hamlet became a district of the larger administrative town or village, and the headman was commonly called *kuchō*, or district chief. Formally, the district chiefs and their deputies were appointed by the municipal council on the recommendation of the mayor of the town or village. In fact, however, the headman selected by the hamlet usually became the district chief. The responsibilities of district chief included both the traditional duties of hamlet government and tasks assigned to him by the municipal administration. Hamlet government duties were diverse and combined an enormous volume of work. The district chief's position was prestigious and he had many responsibilities, but in terms of real power the representatives on the municipal council were in a much stronger position than the district chief, who might not necessarily be chosen from among the most powerful men in the hamlet. Often the district chief became little more than the errand boy of the hamlet council, particularly in hamlets where common forest and field property was important; the officials in control of that property held superior power, relegating the district chief to a secondary role. On the whole, however, in prewar hamlets the district chief held a relatively powerful position.

Hamlets often had a council which acted as an advisory body to the district chief, and its members were known by various names: *hyōgiin*, *kyōgiin*, and *kukai-giin*. Hamlet government was essentially in the hands of the municipal councilmen elected by the hamlet, the district chief, and the hamlet council. In hamlets where there was no formal council, the *kumi* heads performed similar functions. Under the district chief, the heads of the *kumi* were the lowest echelon in the system of information relays from the administrative town or village government to residents. Because it was a consultative and advisory body, the hamlet council was made up of persons from the influential families of the hamlet. In many hamlets, households whose heads were eligible for council positions were firmly fixed in tradition. In the presence of a hamlet council, the position of *kumi* head tended to be perfunctory, and each *kumi* member took his turn as *kumi* head. But where there was no consultative body like the council, the position of the *kumi* head was somewhat like that of the former *kumi-gashira*, a man who wielded great power in hamlet decision-making and would be selected from an influential family in the *kumi*.

Other hamlet administrative groups and positions included the treasurer, the overseer of common lands (*san'ya-iin* or *yama-sōdai*), the irrigation officer (*suiri-iin*), and the public works officer (*doboku-iin*). Not every hamlet had a treasurer. In very small hamlets, or in those with very little treasury business, accounts were handled by the district chief or by his deputy. The officers were appointed only when needed; none of these positions was common to all hamlets. If the duties involved were of great importance to the hamlet, only the most influential members of the hamlet would be chosen to fill the post.

In addition, there were many other positions which, though strictly not official hamlet positions, were treated as such because the hamlet was an undifferentiated community. Good examples are the *ujiko sōdai* and the head of the *wakamono-gumi*, or the chairman of the hamlet agricultural practice union. Similarly regarded were the hamlet representatives of organizations based in the administrative town or village, such as the chief of the fire brigade and the heads of the hamlet youth and women's associations. Members of administrative village committees in charge of taxes, education, or health, or, after the war, the director of the hamlet civic hall or the public welfare officer were all considered hamlet posts. The same was true of the directors (*riji*) and auditors (*kanji*) in Nōkyō before the local municipal amalgamation of 1953. All of these posts were held by only a handful of hamlet residents, many of whom held two or more posts at the same time. For the *buraku*, for example, the chairman of the local agricultural practice union was treated as if he were the chief of the hamlet production department, the director of the local civic hall like the cultural affairs department chief, and the head of the *seinen-dan* like the chief of the youth department. Most hamlets did not, in fact, have such departments, although they did exist in some.

In most cases, hamlet administration was made up of the above-mentioned positions and appointments were made by the *buraku* general assembly. During the Tokugawa period, the general assembly was called the *mura yoriai*, and in form it was the highest decision-making body in the hamlet.

General assembly meetings in the hamlet were scheduled periodically, either in the slack farming season around New Year's or in the spring and fall; but extraordinary meetings were convened whenever an emergency arose or an important problem needed attention. The basic unit of membership in the general assembly was the household rather than the individual, and each household had to send one member, preferably its head. Even today, in most hamlets, the *ie* is the basic unit of assembly membership, and the household head as a rule attends the meetings.

At the regular meetings, replacements are selected for officers whose terms have expired. In most villages, the rule is one-household, one-vote. In the past, officers were not always elected, but decided on by informal agreement among the powerful members of the hamlet whose recommendations were then approved by the assembly. Hamlet finances were also reported at meetings, but very few hamlets submitted their budgets for general approval. Also, as a legislative body, new rules were formulated at hamlet assembly meetings and any changes in scheduled hamlet events would be approved. The assembly also made decisions concerning the use of hamlet-owned facilities, approved the awarding of shares in hamlet property to new members, and deliberated punitive measures to be taken against violators of hamlet rules.

As a rule, all hamlet decisions were unanimous. Just as the villagers considered it best to choose hamlet officials by recommendation, they also insisted on unanimity. Decisions by majority vote would have obstructed hamlet peace and solidarity. While formally the general assembly was the highest decision-making body, in fact most decisions were made by the major power-holders in the hamlet, the council members. As a result, there was little distinction between the legislative and the executive powers. Decisions made by hamlet leaders centering around the district chief were in effect merely approved by the unanimous vote of the assembly.

Of course, *buraku* institutions of self-government have kept pace with social change; the *buraku sōkai* of today is quite different from the *mura yoriai* of the Tokugawa period. The duties and functions of hamlet officials, too, changed not only in name, but in scope and content. The qualifications for official appointments are much different as well. All of these points will be discussed further in the section on changes in hamlet power structure below.

Hamlet Government Operations

Generally speaking, hamlets did not have special offices for the conduct of administrative affairs. Most had some sort of meeting hall, and today, many such halls are designated as the branch of the town or village civic hall. Except in some large hamlets where the volume of work is great, the district chief rarely has his office in the local civic hall, but conducts the affairs of his position in his own home. During his term of office, the district chief has custody of a filing cabinet containing official documents and works together with other hamlet officials in handling the day-to-day affairs of hamlet administration.

Although new rules have been formulated through assembly decision, the conduct of hamlet government follows a prescribed pattern handed down through generations. In some hamlets, customary practices were written down. In a few instances, the hamlet's written by-laws detail not only the rights and obligations of residents, but some of the most minute aspects of village life and often run to several score articles. Other hamlets had several different by-laws, each dealing with a particular problem, rather than a unified set of hamlet regulations. In either case, the writing down of these regulations was intended to prevent the traditional order from further disintegrating and to reaffirm the strength of customary law. However, reasons for writing down village by-laws must be deduced from the conditions in each particular village. Villagers may have come into contact with national law when conflict arose over water rights or when a dispute over use of common lands was taken to court. Such situations probably provided the incentive for eventually codifying customary practices, even though there was no urgent need to do so. The precedents set by hamlets first to do this were undoubtedly studied and used as models by neighboring hamlets. However, hamlets with clearly written by-laws were the exception rather than the rule, and hamlet government had not disintegrated to the point where it could not be conducted without written regulations.

Nevertheless, increased literacy and the weakening of communal solidarity tended to encourage the writing down of hamlet regulations. Many new situations also arose that demanded revision of traditional practices and ways of handling problems. Adjustments were required, for example, when, around the turn of the century, farms were becoming impoverished and the need for thrift and conservation was urgent. Written agreements were made in many hamlets for economies in carrying out marriages, festivals, funerals, and other ceremonies, and to encourage a philosophy of diligence. As hamlet solidarity loosened and farm families began to emphasize their private interests and rights, the arbitrary rule of the hamlet upper class was supplanted, and this became another reason for clearly defining hamlet laws and punishments for violations. There are many examples of written records of punishments and sanctions made particularly in mountain villages.

But such hamlets were the exception; even when new laws were adopted or changes made in old ones, the villagers had little use for written rules. Even if new rules were made, they would simply be recorded in the assembly minutes, but villagers usually remembered the changes without reference to such records.

Largely because of the lack of national legislation to regulate hamlet activities, it is difficult to generalize about rural hamlet government. National law recognized only the administrative district, and not even the names of official positions in the hamlet were recognized, except for the district chief and his deputy. Although the above description holds in most cases, differing local conditions and traditions meant different methods of organizing government, different names for offices and institutions, and different types of administrative procedure.

Despite all this diversity, one practice which widely prevailed was the collection of dues for official purposes. These levies were variously known as *buraku kyōgihi*, *kuhi*, or *ōazahi*, and the 1955 settlement survey shows that 77 percent of all settlements at that time were using such levies. As shown in Table 31, the largest portion of these funds was earmarked for roads, festivals, and officials' allowances. In addition to hamlet dues proper, if one includes the fees simultaneously collected by the main hamlet organization on behalf of other hamlet groups, it becomes clear that many hamlets were also involved in irrigation and production facility financing. Funds for the irrigation union and the agricultural practice union were collected by the hamlet, showing that the hamlet acted as a collection agent for the union. This is itself a sign of increasing, though limited, differentiation between the hamlet and such organizations. As Table 31 shows, though irrigation and agricultural production facilities are of direct benefit only to the individual farmer, such funds were still paid by one-fourth of the hamlets from community coffers. As implied by the term *manzō* (lit., all expenses) used in the Hokuriku region, hamlet levies were generally used for any purpose designated by the hamlet. Already in 1955, however, it was clear that considerable differentiation had occurred in collection of funds between the hamlet organization and groups within it.

Table 31 Items of Hamlet Budget Expenses, 1955 (percent)

Item	For direct expenditure	On behalf of a separate organization in the hamlet for which it acts as collecting agent
Road repairs	54.4	—
Irrigation	24.4	16.7
Production facilities	28.0	8.4
Health and hygiene	35.3	6.1
Road lighting	29.4	—
Festivals	48.2	25.2
Expense allowances for officials	57.2	—

Hamlet dues, of course, are mainly collected from hamlet residents, in some foothill and mountain regions supplemented with income from common field and forest lands. Some hamlets do not collect hamlet dues at all because the income from hamlet-owned assets is sufficient to pay for administrative expenses, but 90 percent of settlements with hamlet budgets do collect hamlet dues in some amount. In general, these dues are assessed in a combination of three methods: in proportion to the amount of farmland owned, based on a scale determined by wealth, and on an equal-amount-per-household basis. For example, funds for festivals of the local deity are collected in equal amounts from each household, funds for irrigation according to the size of a farmer's land, and other fees on a predetermined scale. Most hamlets, however, rather than assessing each type of fee separately, would simply collect a lump sum of which 40 percent was calculated in terms of land owned or farmed, 30 percent on assessed wealth, and 30 percent on an equal amount per household basis. Methods of assessment and collection are now more rational and efficient than before the war, but Table 32, concern-

Table 32   Methods of Collecting Hamlet Fees, 1955 (percent)

Equal contributions of more than 500 yen from each house	7.5
Same, less than 500 yen	23.5
According to " family standing "	8.7
According to size of holding, municipal tax, or income tax	20.8
A combination of more than one of the above methods	39.4

ing the different methods of collection found by the 1955 settlement survey, shows that almost 40 percent of hamlets still combine several types of assessment. Assessment made on the basis of cultivated land area, local tax, or income tax is relatively rational, but not necessarily fair. It is noteworthy that the equal levy method was being used in 31 percent of hamlets, and that in 8.7 percent of villages considerable weight was still given to family status in making assessments by wealth. This problem will be discussed again later; suffice it to say here that hamlet dues weigh heaviest on lower income families even more than do local taxes, which as a rule tend to be harder on the poorer farmer than national income taxes.

In hamlets too small for regular collection of funds, levies might be made only when necessary, or the district chief would cover required expenses out of his own pocket and collect from the villagers later. When the number of households is greater and village expenses are higher, collection is more periodic, and the amount collected is based on the expenditures of the previous year. Nevertheless, few hamlets compile a formal budget and collect funds on that basis. Even in the 1955 survey, the figures show that hamlets using budgeting procedures in the broadest sense amounted to only 53 percent.

Hamlet funds included not only dues collected from residents, but income from hamlet-owned assets and subsidies from the administrative town or village. But only 23 percent of settlements using hamlet funds included the former and only 48 percent included the latter. It should not be overlooked as well that the practice of using income from communal assets for hamlet funds essentially amounts to raising the dues assessed from each household on an equal basis. In addition, when the municipal government provides a subsidy, the hamlet must raise funds of a greater sum than the subsidy for the designated project. Projects that are the responsibility of the village or town administration are often passed on to the hamlet in return for only a small subsidy, a problem which will be discussed further under the subject of the dual burden of taxation.

Another problem of hamlet administration concerns compulsory labor service. Before the money economy became universal, the administration of hamlet affairs required very little cash— probably only enough to purchase office supplies. Most hamlet work could be accomplished with local resources, such as by cutting and hauling timber from the forest, as well as with the uncompensated labor of the villagers. With the development of the commodity economy, the increased need for cash to run community affairs meant a concomitant rise in the number of hamlets collecting membership fees. But the practice of compulsory labor persisted, in what may be called "village work." Uncompensated labor was exacted from the villagers at minimum in the form of road repair and irrigation ditch dredging. Road repair was probably the most common task, usually carried out twice a year in the spring and fall. In the 1955 agricultural settlement survey, 94 percent of all settlements were doing their own road construction and maintenance; of these, almost all (96 percent) required the labor of one person from each household and only 11 percent offered a daily wage. At that time at least, mandatory unpaid labor service was general practice in rural Japan.

As Table 33 shows, in 1955 the survey found that 35 percent of settlements conducted dredging of irrigation ditches with the uncompensated labor of all the villagers. Road maintenance benefits the entire settlement, and dredging of irrigation ditches ought to be the concern only of villagers actually engaged in rice farming, yet the survey shows that, particularly in cases where there is only one irrigation canal, non-farming residents put in just as many days on canal maintenance as farmers.

Table 33 Apportionment of Labor Service for Public Works, 1955 (percent)

	Road Repair	Irrigation Ditch Dredging
Everyone works same amount of time	95.4	35.0
In proportion to land cultivated	2.2	12.5
In proportion to amount of hamlet fees	0.3	—
Hamlet hires workers	0.7	2.3
Beneficiaries only put in equal time	—	41.8
Irrigation union hires workers	—	1.8

The average hamlet required an estimated six days a year of unpaid labor from each household, and along with the equal amount per household assessment of hamlet dues, the practice further aggravated the burden which tended to weigh heavier on poorer families. The fruits of the labor, too, inevitably were enjoyed more by the wealthier members of the hamlet. Dredging of canals and upkeep of farm and mountain roads, when done by the one-household–one-laborer system, were always more beneficial to the wealthier farmer, who made use of those facilities year round, than to the poorer farmer, who had to work to augment his income from non-farm sources during slack seasons. Again, the wealthier farmer uses both irrigation facilities and roads much more than the smaller-scale farmer. Also, due to the financial constraints under which administrative villages or towns labor, unpaid hamlet labor may be used not only for periodic tasks like road repair, but for many other jobs. When the administrative village does not have sufficient funds for public works projects for which it is responsible, it manages with unpaid labor, rationalizing it on the pretext that the local beneficiaries should shoulder the burden.

The contradictions inherent in hamlet government grew more conspicuous as individual farm operation increasingly diverged from the self-sufficient, communal system of production. But as long as farm families were unable to break away completely from that system, hamlet government had to retain many of its traditional practices, be it in the assessment of hamlet dues or in the system of obligatory labor. Since hamlet government was conditioned by the structure of stratification in the hamlet, its contradictions included potential conflicts between strata. This latent conflict had existed in the communal village. Though the early tenant farmer carried an excessive burden in uncompensated labor he received various benefits and protection through the paternalism of the landlord which ameliorated inter-strata relations. But the structural changes that have taken place since modernization began have affected relations among the strata, making it impossible to hide the contradictions inherent in the traditional system of self-government. Although the hamlet did retain some of its former legal sanctions as well as the authority to punish violators of hamlet rules or those who deviated from accepted norms, its power to enforce was greatly weakened. Since ostracism, or the deprivation of rights known as *murahachibu*, no longer carried the authority it once did, hamlet government could not be conducted on the basis of traditional customs with their inherent potential for inter-strata conflict. Potential conflict had to be gradually alleviated and administration rationalized in response to the needs of changing times.

Changes in Hamlet Government

As families in the hamlet became more autonomous and less homogeneous, the conflicts and contradictions of hamlet government were clearly evident. When the livelihood of every family had been guaranteed if it submitted to the communal production system, and when relations between upper-class landlord and lower-class tenants were that of patron and servant, hamlet people were forced to suppress individual interests in conformity with the demands of hamlet government. But with the growth of the commodity economy, farmers took a keener view of the benefits and losses of their economic activities. As private, independent management of farm production grew, hamlet government could no longer function as it had. New elements of dysfunction emerged in government as the hamlet community became further stratified, and increasing numbers of farmers deriving income from non-farm sources created a new class not totally dependent on farming for their livelihood. Thus the hamlet is much more heterogeneous than it was when every family made its living by farming. Even in the mountain areas where the proportion of farmers has remained fairly stable, the hamlet is now less unified. The price for timber and forest products has risen, but only those who originally held rights to timberlands benefit, and all newcomers are excluded, a situation which has had severe repercussions on village unity because it splits residents into factions of those who do and do not hold rights to forest land. In such villages, reforms have been necessary to allow hamlet government to function effectively.

In addition to the difficulty in resolving the contradictions which arose from the gap between hamlet strata, an unavoidable estrangement existed between the hamlet administration that carried over from the traditional village government and the new institutions of the administrative village. The situation became acute during the post–World War II period, due not only to rapid changes in hamlet structure but to attitudinal shifts among farmers. Hamlet government had to change, and attention will now be focused on how that change evolved in both organization and management.

First, with regard to changes in hamlet administration, was the decline in the prestige and authority of the district chief. In most hamlets, the honor of holding this post had been second only to that of being on the administrative village assembly, and all these positions were held by persons of prominence for considerably long periods of time. The district chief was in charge of all aspects of hamlet government and usually had assistants to help and run errands in the performance of these duties. But as times changed, fewer people were willing to do the menial tasks of a messenger, so that the district chief was often forced to do all the contacting and negotiating among village residents himself. Although the post had once been honorary, it became necessary to provide the district chief with a stipend. More and more organizations were formed in the hamlet, and since one person could hold only a limited number of posts and all of the new organizations had different heads, the district chief could no longer oversee all the affairs of the hamlet. Moreover, his time was practically monopolized by the affairs of the administrative village, a trend which reached its height during World War II when the hamlet chief was inundated with the work of conveying central and prefectural government orders to the members of his village. In the postwar period, with the abolition of the *tonari-gumi* system, the term "district chief" fell into temporary disuse, and the holder of the position was known as the *renraku-in* (liaison officer) or the *chūzai-in* (local officer). At that stage, the holder of this office became even more like that of an administrative messenger. In many hamlets the prestige and authority of the district chief declined, and he was forced to take on ever more menial tasks. People who once coveted this position now tried to avoid selection.

The hamlet council, too, was less and less occupied by people of influence. While the district chief became something of a common clerk, the positions on the council came to resemble that of *kumi* head, and all official positions declined markedly in prestige and authority. In areas where neighboring hamlets shared the rights to forest and field lands which were a source of income for the hamlet, an influential person was needed to negotiate with the other hamlets, and the *yama-sōdai* position might hold considerable authority. Yet, generally speaking, though hamlet officials carried an even heavier burden, they ceased to hold the unreserved respect of villagers. Appointment to village administrative posts was determined no longer by the recommendation of influential hamlet leaders, but by formal election, probably made necessary by the decline in prestige of these positions. Most significant, however, was the change in thinking of the average hamlet resident. All these changes became even more conspicuous and definite after the postwar land reform.

The hamlet general assembly was no longer only the occasion for approving the decisions of village elders. The *mura yoriai* of former times, where hamlet families held seats of prominence according to family status and lower class members sat quietly in the background, gradually changed. Now dissent frequently occurs at assembly meetings and unanimous decisions are often very difficult to reach. Again, this trend grew especially noticeable after the land reform. The tradition of one-household–one-vote still continues, but in some areas the one-person–one-vote system is also gaining popularity. Under these changed circumstances it no longer suffices to make a simple budget report. Now it is necessary to submit the budget for general approval. Where once personal interests were sacrificed for the group, it is now necessary to take various individual interests into account. This same trend is behind the growing separation between the hamlet and the organizations within it. Attendance at the assembly is no longer mandatory, and if the problems before the assembly are not considered important, many people will not attend, making it difficult to hold a productive session.

In general, methods of raising hamlet funds have been rationalized. As the statistics in Table 32 show, in 1955 the practice of collecting an equal amount from each household, despite its inherent "false equality," was still widespread. Although neither rational nor fair, this method was still a great improvement on the system of determining payments on the basis of household wealth and status. Equal assessment, in fact, grew more common in the postwar period, which may at first seem retrogressive. Yet, one must remember that despite the relatively light burden on each family in the upper strata, the prewar system made poorer families feel obligated because the amount paid by the upper strata, at least in absolute terms, was larger, and this persuaded the less powerful to submit to the will of the upper strata. After the war, equal levies were often preferred because that method allowed everyone an equal voice in hamlet affairs.

As we have seen, even today the practice is widespread for the hamlet to act as the collecting agent for hamlet organizations in addition to raising its own dues. In such cases, however, organizational fees are assessed separately, and if the number of cases where hamlet organizations collect their own fees is considered together with this, it is clear that these organizations are tending to break away from hamlet control. The tendency to abandon the lump sum assessment of both hamlet dues and specialized fees is also another sign of rationalization.

Change has taken place in the handling of "village work" as well. Once an accepted duty, today this kind of uncompensated service can no longer be taken for granted. In 1955, of 94 percent of settlements conducting periodic road repair, 96 percent

Table 34 Compensation for Repair Work on Public Roads,
1970 (percent)

Every household required to provide labor	53.1
Cash compensation required of non-participants	17.8
Daily allowances paid to the participants	2.8
Workers hired	0.2
Not under hamlet control	26.1

relied on uncompensated hamlet labor. The 1970 census figures presented in Table 34, however, show that the number of hamlets responsible for local road repair had dropped to 74 percent, and in only half the settlements were all households contributing labor for such projects. Clearly the number of villages that do their own road maintenance has greatly decreased, and the decline is even more marked in the dredging and maintenance of irrigation ditches, a communal task in only 64 percent of settlements according to the 1970 census. Today residents volunteer only reluctantly to do tasks in which the entire village once pooled their efforts because the tasks were of benefit to everyone. Now village work is known as the most inefficient form of labor, and the hamlet must make special efforts to get residents to participate. Those who cannot help at the scheduled time may be assigned to work at a later date or asked to make a cash contribution. As social change has loosened the unity of the hamlet, persons who do not perform the work they are expected to are more often quietly excused, as reflected in Table 35 compiled from the 1955 survey.

Table 35 Action against Failure to Perform Hamlet
Tasks, 1955 (percent)

No official action taken	32.6
Work required later	15.7
Fine collected	37.0
Other measures	1.3
No precedent of failure	13.5

The number of non-farm families living in the hamlet has increased, and it is difficult to require village work of these families despite the fact that they use village roads as much as anyone. The proportion of hamlets requiring services of the non-farmer was 82 percent in 1955, but it has become very difficult to continue this practice. One reflection of this is in the rising number of villages which no longer require any communal labor at all. Inevitably, hamlets are being forced to shift away from reliance on uncompensated labor and provide a token wage for work done. Naturally, such wages are very low compared to the standard for similar work, but the number of villages which do pay seems to be increasing. The 1970 census shows that 2 percent of hamlets were paying wages for road repair, and 3 percent for irrigation ditch dredging. These are very low figures, but the percentages suggest that there are many more hamlets which, though they pay no cash wages, often deduct a certain amount from hamlet dues for service rendered.

Underlying the changes in hamlet government is the change in the structure of the hamlet as a rural community, the changing system of stratification and occupational diversification. More will be said about stratification later; in connection with occupational diversification, an important change to note is the gradual split away from the hamlet of the agricultural practice unions and the irrigation unions. The hamlet no longer plays an all-embracing role, and its inability to do so is closely related to changes in hamlet self-government.

For a long time after the Meiji Restoration, the hamlet took care of all its own basic expenses, as its Tokugawa period predecessors had done, including administrative costs and expenses for the local shrine, shrine festivals, road maintenance, and other public works as well as those for irrigation, agricultural production, fire fighting, public health, taxes on hamlet-owned assets, and electricity for street lights and hamlet-owned buildings. The hamlet relied on unpaid labor for any aspect of village work it could, but as the number of non-farmers increased, it became more difficult to use funds collected from everyone for agricultural production costs, farm production facilities, irrigation, and water costs. It became only logical for the irrigation union to collect fees for irrigation, the agricultural practice union for expenses related to farming and for production costs.

As this trend progresses, control over hamlet assets tends to break away from the hamlet as well. People with rights to the use of fields and forests form their own special groups separate from the hamlet. Even if they do not form a property corporation, they become independent enough to refuse the use of the revenues from those assets for hamlet government purposes. This process of differentiation appears to be an inevitable part of hamlet rationalization.

As the hamlet and its functional organizations become more differentiated, the hamlet will become a purely administrative district in the formal sense. Already today, more emphasis is given to work for the administrative district than to that of the hamlet itself. Consequently, if the *buraku* is no longer required as an administrative unit of village government, and as the organizations within the hamlet completely divest themselves of hamlet control, hamlet self-government will be left only with minimal routine tasks required by small neighborhood groups. Hamlet funds will eventually be absorbed into funds for private groups and for the financing of the public municipality.

Despite the tendency for functional groups to go their separate ways, the hamlet is still a comprehensive governmental unit. This is partly because structural breakdown is not yet complete and partly because people still cling to old ways of thinking on how the hamlet ought to be run. It is also because the municipality requires a comprehensive governmental unit like the hamlet. The administrative hamlet was never legally institutionalized. Still, the municipality continued to use the hamlet as an administrative district even after the postwar reforms. Along with subsidies to the hamlet administrative district, the municipality uses the hamlet as a relay for administrative information, a pattern which remains unchanged from before the amalgamation of local government units in 1953. It could be argued that the hamlet unit has become even more important for this administrative function since the amalgamation produced ever-larger municipalities. The municipal government use of the hamlet tends to support its dual character, for the hamlet must continue its function as both an administrative district and an overall framework for the organizations within the hamlet itself, even though they are no longer identifiable with the hamlet as a whole. Complete separation between hamlet association and agricultural practice union is seen only in those hamlets which are close to the large urban areas, where the non-farm population has increased to the extent that total separation of farm-oriented organizations is mandatory. Even in 1970, when the census showed that the number of non-farmers had overwhelmingly surpassed farmers, only 4 percent of hamlets gave separate consideration to non-farm families in local administration. In most hamlets, the process of differentiation is by no means smooth, making residual contradictions in hamlet government that much more apparent.

Relations between municipal and hamlet government will be discussed in Chapter Four. But before going on, an overall examination should be made of the power structure which supported hamlet government.

The Power Structure of the Hamlet

Social Stratification in the Prewar Hamlet

The 1970 agricultural census shows that in 42 percent of settlements in the early Shōwa era, 70 percent or more of the farmers were tenants. In 30 percent of the settlements, more than 70 percent of farmers owned and worked their own farms, and in 26 percent of the settlements, the majority of farmers operated both rented land and their own fields. Of settlements made up primarily of tenant farmers, about 20 percent were dominated by landlords with large holdings of 50 hectares or more, while in the remaining four-fifths of the settlements the landlords' holdings were less than 50 hectares. Among the latter group of smaller landlords, slightly over half lived in the settlement and half elsewhere. The composition of the prewar hamlets was varied, including some that were made up largely of farmers working their own land without great differences between the social strata. Every hamlet included a number of tenants and even where they were in the majority, there were also owner-operators. When most of the farmers were tenants and the landlord did not reside in the village, he appointed one farm family to act as his agent.

While patterns of ownership varied widely, some broad generalizations can be made about stratification in the prewar hamlet. Usually there were one or two major landlords and about one-third of local farmers operated their own land, another third both farmed their own land and rented land from the landlord, and the final third were wholly tenant operators.

These patterns of owner-tenant stratification were intertwined with branch and stem family, as well as *oyakata* and *kokata*, relations. In the typical village, the landlord family, simultaneously the stem family and the *oyakata*, stood at the peak of the hierarchy. Immediately below the landlord were the owner-farmers, who formed the upper-middle stratum of the hamlet. They included the immediate branch families of the stem, the stem families of minor *dōzoku* groups, and the *kokata* of the top *oyakata* who were themselves the *oyakata* of *kokata* on levels below them. On the lower-middle and lower strata were the part-owners and tenant farmers. These families were the "grandchild branches," two steps removed from the landlord, and might also be branches of the minor *dōzoku* groups, as well as *kokata* clients of lesser *oyakata*. In many hamlets the status hierarchy was reflected in the way children addressed their parents. Children in the highest stratum called their fathers *otōsan*, and in the upper-middle, *otō*, in the middle, *tete*, while those on the bottom rungs used the word *dede*. These distinctions were of great significance, serving to sharply differentiate people according to status and prestige.

The complexity of relations which resulted from the overlap of stem-branch family and *oyakata-kokata* bonds meant that the connection between landlord and tenant was not simply a payment of rent for the use of land. If the tenant family suffered misfortune or financial difficulty, the landlord, who might also be the tenant's stem family or his *oyakata*, would lend him assistance. If there was a crop failure or poor harvest, the landlord would distribute rice and other grains to tenant families from his own stores. Landlords also served as guarantors for loans from the mutual finance associations (*mujin-kō*) and at times gave gifts of saké to his *kokata* or tenants. To repay these favors, the tenant frequently helped out at the landlord's house, and responded without hesitation whenever the landlord called for assistance; relationships between superior and subordinate thus functioned in an atmosphere of familism. Exploitation was an inherent part of landlord-tenant ties, but it was softened by the benevolence of *oyakata-kokata* and stem-branch relations. The social strata were patterned in a hierarchy of superior and sub-ordinate relations, but those relations were also familistic.

Of course, this typical pattern existed in only a few villages. In villages where forms of stratification had survived since feudal times and where the landlord had preserved his power as a local magnate, the pattern was strong. But even during the Tokugawa period, few villages came close to the ideal type, and after the beginning of the Meiji era, they became even rarer. This is suggested, as mentioned above, by the results of the 1955 survey which indicated that only 12 percent of settlements were characterized by the customary exchange of labor centered around the needs of the *oyakata* or stem family.

Even in hamlets made up of the tenant farmers of a merchant-moneylender landlord with a large estate, there were smaller landlords who worked their own land. These lesser landowners, who served simultaneously as agents for the larger landlords, became the upper stratum of village society. Even in villages composed of farmers who became landowners through diligence and thrift, a distinct status ranking existed—landlord, owner-farmer, part-owner, tenant—which demonstrated the qualities of the hierarchical social structure. Landlord-tenant relations were further complicated by the bonds of mutual assistance and cooperative labor, buttressed by the traditional ties between upper and lower strata, and interwoven into the hierarchical social order by economic power and family status.

As the capitalist economy developed, inexorably penetrating the patterns of village life and stimulating the production of the farms, the intricate social order gradually began to break down. The landlords, who had been the core of the hamlet's hierarchical order, grew parasitic, living off the fruits of the land produced by others but losing their direct ties with the land and the local people. The pattern of change was not uniform in every hamlet. Although perhaps oversimplified, there were two general patterns. One type occurred in regions where the increase in agricultural productivity remained low and industrialization had not spread. The other was found in regions where productivity was higher than the first type and where industrialization had considerably progressed. In these two types of areas, the breakdown of the hierarchical social order occurred in a different manner.

Moreover, since in the former areas of poor agricultural productivity and low industrialization, clear examples of the typical pattern of social stratification as described above were more numerous, and the gap between these two types widened.

In an earlier work, I described these two patterns as the *dōzoku* (a hierarchical structure) and the *kōgumi* (a horizontally oriented structure centered on the *kō* and/or *kumi*). They have also been called the "northeastern" and "southwestern" patterns. But because the terms northeastern and southwestern imply a clear geographical difference, and many examples of the northeastern pattern can, in fact, be seen in the southwest and vice-versa, I prefer to avoid possible confusion by referring to them here as the "developed" and "underdeveloped" village types.

In the underdeveloped areas the industrial structure was still primitive, and transportation and communication facilities were inadequate, making it difficult for local residents to move to jobs outside the hamlet. This situation applied to both landlord and tenant classes. The money economy had not thoroughly penetrated these areas, and development of commercial agriculture was difficult, so that farms tended to produce primarily on a subsistence basis. Horizontal social mobility in these areas as well as vertical mobility between the economic strata was sluggish, and the social order remained much as it had always been. The landlords who stood at the apex of the social hierarchy had few opportunities to shift into other fields of endeavor or even to leave the area and become parasitic landlords. Many reduced their directly cultivated holdings, but remained on the land as farming landlords. These landlords who continued to operate their farms employed small farmers in the village and continued to be closely involved in and concerned with village life. They retained close contact with village people and thereby helped to perpetuate the traditional structure of stratification.

The social hierarchy was also reinforced by the communal nature of the hamlet. In such hamlets, the farmers relied heavily on the hamlet supply of fertilizer and mulch, and control over commonly held field and forest lands was not relinquished, another factor that sustained the "village community" aspects of the hamlet. In general, irrigation facilities in these areas were rarely modernized, and communal control of the water supply was strong. The low level of agricultural productivity preserved communal work organizations of various types, such as those for mending and thatching roofs, and meant that the festivals and sharing of food and drink that took the place of entertainment in the countryside retained their importance. Overlapping co-operative patterns strengthened communal pressures and fore-stalled the dissolution of the traditional customs of daily life interwoven into the hierarchical social structure.

By contrast, in the developed settlements, the growth of local industries led to the emergence of a more advanced and complex industrial structure. Communication and transportation devel-oped, facilitating contact with other localities as well as greater occupational mobility. The upper landlord strata here, different from their counterparts in underdeveloped areas, benefited from the education brought within their reach by their increased economic power, and they were able to move into other jobs, some becoming complete parasites with no direct involvement in agriculture. The lower ranks of the tenant farmers also left the farm in search of a better life in the city. Meanwhile, a new type of farmer appeared among those who remained in the village, who farmed part-time and commuted to work elsewhere to ob-tain extra income. The social mobility of the farmer was mark-edly increased on the horizontal plane in local areas, and since the money economy spread rapidly in these developed areas, vertical mobility was also considerable. The social hierarchy had never been rigid in rural areas, and socioeconomic changes loosened it even more. As modernization proceeded, landlords who had already ceased farming their own lands began to leave the hamlet in greater numbers. Even those who retained resi-dence in the hamlet usually worked in a nearby urban area and lost their direct involvement in rural life. The fortunes of the entire landlord strata underwent great fluctuations, and so their traditional status and authority tended to decline. A new stratum of farming landlords arose to take their place, but the newcomers did not have the power to maintain or revitalize the traditional social hierarchy.

Communal rules in advanced hamlets weakened. Agricultural productivity increased, and farmers relied more and more on commercially produced fertilizers. Eventually the hamlet-owned fields and forests were divided among residents. Higher agricultural productivity rendered many cooperative labor groups unnecessary, leading to their eventual disbandment. Modern civil engineering techniques were used to rebuild irrigation facilities, and gradually the communal control and management of irrigation became less important. Increased contacts with urban society brought more opportunities for entertainment, decreasing the importance of community-sponsored festivals, pot-luck dinners, and drinking parties. The breakdown of the self-sufficient, isolated rural community, coupled with the changes in the system of stratification, meant that much of the rigidity of the social hierarchy relaxed.

As we have seen, the stratification system differed from region to region, and the same was true of the degree of change. In general, however, the tendency for landlords to become parasitic was nationwide, and even in underdeveloped areas, the incoming tide of capitalism could not be put off, bringing about the inevitable breakdown of the traditional social hierarchy.

Still, as long as the landlord system continued to exist, the hierarchical character of the community would, while changing gradually, persist. Former landlords might move off the farm and become more parasitic, but they were supplanted by farming landlords, and the division between owner and tenant continued so that a new, more rational system could not be established in its place. Even in hamlets where social rank was not formally recognized and economic power and the ability of the individual were considered most important, a strong consciousness of family status continued to prevail. In most hamlets the customary social patterns of status weakened but were not entirely eliminated.

Stratification in the Postwar Hamlet

The postwar period brought vast changes in social stratification. The most important catalyst of this change was the agricultural land reform, undertaken in 1946. The effects of the reform were not uniform throughout the nation. In the underdeveloped villages the landlords who had stayed actively involved in farming were able to sustain their power after the reform. In the developed areas the landlords who had become parasitic lost all of their land and all of their power as well. The former, however, could not uphold the authority they had once enjoyed. Nevertheless, they, as well as the owner-cultivators in the developed areas, were firmly entrenched in the upper strata of hamlet society. The owner-farmers and part-owners were able to augment their holdings as a result of the land reform and their economic power was strengthened, shrinking the gap between themselves and the strata above them.

The landlord stratum lost its position at the apex of the social hierarchy but shared it with the upper-middle-class farmer, and ex-landlords could not maintain their central position in stem-branch relationships. Customs built up over generations were not suddenly abandoned, and branch families continued to extend various courtesies to their stem family. These were reciprocated; the stem family still invited all branch members to periodic banquets and retained other practices, although gifts of saké presented from time to time as a gesture of good will were generally discontinued. Since the labor groups which had centered on the stem family were gradually collapsing, traditional customs and courtesies were carried on by inertia, and, given the opportunity, they were simply brought to an end. The *oyakata's* social status, essential to maintaining the *oyakata-kokata* relationship, could no longer be maintained; when the help of the *kokata* was no longer needed by the *oyakata*, the relationships were eventually dissolved. Even today, the degree of dissolution of these bonds is faster in the developed than in the underdeveloped areas, but the difference is not as great as it was during the prewar period. Social stratification in most hamlets in Japan is now somewhat like that of the prewar hamlet in the developed areas, where no single large landlord was resident.

Postwar increases in productivity led to the dismantling of communal labor organizations. Urbanization penetrated farm areas, transforming ancient customs and traditions. When the communal nature of the village which had supported the status structure weakened, the collapse of the landlord system brought further erosion to the system of social stratification.

It need not be repeated that land reform did not equalize the system of stratification in the hamlets or narrow the gap between large and small farms. The reform transferred rights to landownership, but did not equalize the size of holdings. Rented lands were generally sold to the tenant who had cultivated them. The part-owner/part-tenants became economically stronger as a result of the reform, but though they gained ownership of the small plots they had cultivated, they were unable to improve their productivity. The structure of stratification shifted from a landlord-tenant pattern to one based on the amount of land owned and cultivated. The old social hierarchy gave way to a new one determined almost totally by economic criteria.

In this sense, there was little significant change in the stratification of rural society. Landlords and owner-farmers alike cultivated the land. The upper strata were reduced in status, but not much change occurred among the lower strata, and the farmer at the lowest rungs remained at the bottom. The major difference was that the landlord was not supreme over them as he had once been. During the period of economic recovery in the first half of the 1950s, there were few opportunities for farmers to work in non-farm occupations, so that the size of the farmer's holdings was the decisive factor in determining his social standing. Those with extensive fields were in the upper stratum, while the small poor farmer remained in the lowest stratum.

More than fifteen years of rapid economic growth have transformed rural stratification into a very complex pattern. It is now difficult to assess a family's economic status solely on the basis of the size of the land it farms. One example is the livestock or fruit farmer who does not require extensive landholdings yet may bring in a large income. Some farmers supplement their income through dairy and poultry products, or by cultivating hothouse vegetables. Another perhaps more important factor which has transformed stratification patterns is the greater access to non-farm income. A farm household's economic position is determined to an even greater degree by the stability and size of its non-farm incomes. A comparison of per capita household expenditures of urban and rural workers can be made from the statistics presented in Table 36. In 1960, the highest per capita farming expenditures were for the landowners of 2.0 hectares and above, but by 1965, the greatest expenditure was by farmers with 0.5 hectares or less, and the gap has been widening ever since.

Today, the family which farms 1 hectare or less has per capita expenses greater than the average for urban workers, those farming 2 hectares or more are below the urban average, and those with 1 to 2 hectares, once the upper-middle stratum of farm society, are in the lowest position of all.

Table 36   Per Capita Household Expenditures for Farm Families According to Size of Land Worked (per capita expenditure for non-farm workers' families = 100)

Year	Farm Families	≤0.5 ha	≤1.0 ha	≤1.5 ha	≤2.0 ha	≥2.0 ha
1960	75.8	79.8	72.5	73.4	77.4	87.4
1965	82.7	86.5	79.5		78.7	83.5
1970	95.3	106.2	93.1	89.7	86.8	90.3
1975	107.1	117.3	107.8	97.6	95.0	98.0

Per capita household expenses depend on accessibility to places of additional employment and are determined in part by whether the farmer lives in an area where industry is sufficiently developed so that farmers can find stable employment. It also depends on whether the land is flat or mountainous and upon its proximity to urban areas. The prewar structure of stratification has greatly changed in the urban, flatland areas where income is more important than farm size, but it remains much the same in more remote regions where the size of holdings determines a farmer's social standing. Now full-time farmers make up only one-tenth of the nation's total, suggesting that part-time farming is becoming the rule even in underdeveloped areas and that stratification patterns are changing there, too.

The basis of rural social stratification has thus shifted from area of land owned to the amount of land actually farmed, and more recently again to level of income. Property size cannot be completely discounted, however, and questions of family status, which have traditionally been connected with landownership and family lineage, continue to figure in the contract of marriages, although less prominently than in the past. Nevertheless more than 30 years after World War II, members of the younger generation in most hamlets have no notion of what their family's former position in the hierarchy was, and even for older people, that era may be a fading memory. Today, total family income, including that from non-farm sources, is important, and although field size may come into consideration when calculating assets, it is no longer the major determinant of family status.

Changes in Hamlet Power Structure

The Tokugawa village was governed by the *jikata-san'yaku*, a group of three leaders consisting of the *nanushi*, the *kumi-gashira*, and the *hyakushōdai*. The position of *nanushi* was usually taken by the head of the village's most powerful family and held by that family for generations. When no single family was supreme, several took turns in the position of *nanushi*. The second level leadership, the *kumi-gashira*, and the third level, the *hyakushōdai*, were also hereditary positions held by families just below the *nanushi* in social status. Another name for this group of leaders was *osabyakushō*, the "senior farmers" of the hamlet, and their position was assured as long as the family continued to provide a male heir. In some cases a few families with distinguished pedigrees maintained a tight hold on the reins of village government. The *osabyakushō* ruled the *komaebyakushō*, petty farmers, and the lowest class of peasants, the *mizunomibyakushō* below them, and all lived in the grip of established communal customs and traditions.

Although the names were changed, the leadership and organization remained much the same after the Meiji Restoration. The village *sōdai* or *kochō* (the latter abolished with the 1889 local government law), were identical to the *nanushi*, just as the people who became village or town assemblymen in the new local government system were drawn from the landlord class. The *kuchō*, or district chief, almost always came from a family ranking just below the landlord and the *nanushi*. The tradition of upper-class families holding village offices was considerably prolonged; they continued to serve in official village positions until well after the Meiji era.

The stem-cum-*oyakata*-cum-landlord families were also, as we have seen, the patrons and rulers of the *buraku*. The families of the upper and middle strata dominated the position of *kuchō* and on the hamlet council and formed an exclusive ruling elite. The part-owners and tenants of the lower strata, dependent as they

were on the economic strength of the upper strata, had to submit to the established rule without dissent, partly because of their
need to rely on cooperative labor and use hamlet-owned assets.
The village assembly of the Tokugawa period, the *mura yoriai*,
became the *buraku sōkai*, which functioned as the highest decision-making body in form only, since it basically only approved
the decisions made beforehand by the ruling class.

Power patterns changed somewhat after the initiation of the
municipal system, partly because of other factors involved in the
process of modernization, but the basic patterns of the feudal
period remained intact, particularly in the undeveloped areas
until the end of World War II. The hamlet council was monopolized by the handful of families at the top of the social system,
and even should a leading family be wiped out or ruined, it
would be replaced by another. The standard for membership
continued to be determined by the amount of land held. The
candidates for administrative village or town assembly were usually known in advance, but if not, the ruling members would
gather to decide. They also essentially appointed the district
chief and the position was usually held by one person for many
years. Other hamlet official positions were held by persons recommended by the council, usually one of the council members.
The majority of villagers could not oppose any council decision
and protest would have meant ostracism or total expulsion from
the hamlet. If disruptions of hamlet life or power struggles took
place, it was only among the members of the ruling stratum; no
leeway was permitted in which the lower strata might revolt
against the upper.

Nevertheless, such villages, in which the family status of the
ruling elite of the village remained absolutely fixed until the
end of World War II, were not necessarily the rule. Changes in
the power structure had occurred throughout the early decades
of this century. These changes were most remarkable in villages
where upper-class *oyakata* lost their family fortunes in the wake
of the economic dislocations of the latter part of the nineteenth
century and were forced to find work outside the village. Even
where the economic position of the *oyakata* was more stable, the
adoption of universal manhood suffrage in 1925 gave the nation
a much broader electorate. As the gap between the enfranchized

citizen and other citizens narrowed and then completely disappeared, it became impossible to maintain the hereditary ruling prerogative of the upper strata. For example, demands were made that middle- and lower-strata representatives in the form of *komaesōdai* be included in the membership of the hamlet council, which was formed to take the place of the hereditary *omodachi*, or "prominent" families. Class tension and confrontation appeared for the first time with the formation of farmers' unions and in the movement for democratization of hamlet government. Many prominent men who held their positions merely on the strength of their hereditary prerogative had to leave office, and middle-class farmers were able to gain a more effective hold on hamlet offices.

As the capitalist economy developed, landlords tended to live off the land, a trend which, coupled with the increased economic power of the part-owner farmer, further transformed the structure of village power. By the turn of the century, compulsory education had increased literacy to the point that members of the middle stratum of farmers were fully qualified to manage the affairs of hamlet government. Under the law, all male adults in the hamlet were given equal status as citizens, and with the adoption of universal manhood suffrage, the hereditary claims of the ruling class to hamlet government positions were totally without effect.

De facto power, however, remained in the hands of the upper strata. Little or no salary was paid for hamlet administrative positions because they were traditionally honorary, and only the farmer of high social status had the time and the financial leeway to allow him to undertake such jobs. Even if the largest landowners left the hamlet, village government was still controlled by farmers who operated their own land and rented some portions to others, and these farmers further benefited by acting as agents for the parasitic landlords. In the top echelon of village society, farmer-landlords and landlord agents manipulated the communal character of the village for their own ends and became the effective rulers of the hamlet. Their contribution to hamlet funds, although a relatively small percentage of the total, was, in absolute terms, large enough to ensure their authority. Since the size of one's contribution to hamlet funds determined the extent of his voice in hamlet affairs, if a middle-class family could contribute an amount comparable to the upper-class family, he was included in the pool of those qualified for village appointments.

The postwar land reform changed the situation even more. The upper-upper class was brought down to the same level as the upper class, inflating its ranks and eliminating great power differences among the members of the upper strata. Abolition of landlord-tenant, *oyakata-kokata*, and stem-branch family relations further reduced upper-class power and with it a reduction in hierarchical authority. Farmers' unions, which had been formed expressly to campaign for the land reform, completely vanished after the reform became effective, although not without having first profoundly shaken the established system of social stratification. In most villages, the class struggle of the union movement was suppressed with relative ease by evoking the importance of hamlet peace and harmony. Any movement based on class solidarity which might draw in other villages and threaten the peace and security of the hamlet was sure to earn the suspicion of every farmer. This is one reason the farmers' union movement never took on a purely class-oriented nature and why, once the reform was implemented, the unions gradually faded out of the picture. Such movements would never have emerged had there been no class opposition to the social order ruled over by the landlords. The demise of landlord power was ultimately brought by the land reform, but it could not have been achieved without the powerful impact of the farmers' unions.

Anti-landlord movements did not take place in every village, and although most rural people did not thoroughly understand the meaning of the new democracy that postwar reform had brought, there was a new spirit of populism in the villages which made it difficult to unify the village into a tight unit around the core of upper-class families. At hamlet council meetings, lower-strata farmers began to express their opinions. Office holders were not chosen as easily as before and many qualified people actually avoided appointment. In some cases villagers took turns as the head of their *kumi*. The hereditary right to positions on the hamlet council became rare even in the underdeveloped regions.

Village leadership not only no longer carried its former authority and prestige, hamlet members ceased to submissively obey the orders made by their superiors. Official power declined somewhat, but those positions were regarded as prestigious, at least in the first 15 years of the postwar period, especially by those who had never served in such a capacity before and had gained the social position and power to do so through the land reform. Size of income became the determining factor of social rank, so that it was not in the interest of most farmers to put their agricultural and other work aside in order to take on the duties of a hamlet administrator, and the tendency to avoid hamlet administration grew, especially among upper-class farmers.

But the hamlet is still an agricultural settlement, and important posts cannot be left to persons whose basic interest is not in farming, such as the part-time farmer whose main income comes from a non-farm source. Ultimately, official posts still go to owners of large-scale farms. These posts are rotated among the farmers, who are forced to take them when their turn comes around. The household who has many farm hands to help with the work is also the most desirable candidate for time-consuming hamlet administrative positions, such as district chief. It is also difficult to select capable, qualified persons for such positions. Able, young people do not want the district chief job because of the enormous burden it involves and because the salary provided jointly by the administrative village and the hamlet is so meager. Thus those most often selected for the chief's job are elderly, conservative in their thinking, and unaccustomed to democratic government. This means that although the social system and life styles have greatly changed, actual administration of the hamlet tends toward the traditional. Even if people dislike the way things are being run, they withhold criticism because the district chief has, after all, forsaken his farm work for hamlet duties, and remuneration for his labors is so negligible.

In contrast to official hamlet positions, agricultural practice union jobs are usually held by men in the prime of life, technically very able and with good management ability. The leadership of groups is now held by different individuals, reflecting the diffusion of hamlet control, and there are few who want to hold more than one position at a time. Power in the village is no longer concentrated in a few hands, and village leadership is more diversified. As the hamlet and the organizations within it gradually drifted apart in administration, settlement control is no longer centralized, and hamlet government under the direction of the district chief can no longer unify residents into a single group. The hamlet is also more heterogeneous, composed of full-time farmers, part-time farmers, and persons with no involvement in farming at all. The hamlet leader functions only within the official confines of his job and cannot exercise his authority in other areas. Although today's hamlet leaders often come from upper-class families, they are not as authoritarian as the prewar landlord.

Upper-class farmers continue to lead the hamlet. Their rule is sustained by the fact that they often serve as the agents of the administrative village or town and for groups whose membership encompasses several hamlets. Another sustaining factor is the persisting belief of hamlet people in the supreme importance of "village harmony." In a survey I conducted in 1968 on change in farmers' attitudes during the postwar period (see Table 37), when asked what they would do if they disagreed with most other people on hamlet administration, the majority of the respondents said that they would express their opinion, but not so strongly as to upset the harmony of the hamlet. More than 70 percent, including both those who said "I would not speak up" and "A person should not assert his personal opinion too much" expressed this attitude. Obviously, although the social structure of the hamlet is more diversified, considerable cohesion still exists

Table 37 Expression of Opinion on Hamlet Government, 1968 (percent)

	Akita	Okayama
Will express my opinion openly even if disruptive to hamlet harmony	23.9	13.2
Will express my opinion as long as it does not disrupt hamlet harmony	53.4	62.5
I would not speak up	3.6	6.6
A person should not assert his personal opinion too much	15.0	15.7
Other	1.7	1.0
Don't know	2.4	1.0

between hamlet administration and village groups. Hamlet government still retains much of its traditional outlook, and it seems unlikely that the village will change in the foreseeable future from the traditional to a new community formed on the basis of rational elections and democratic leadership.

In recent years, nostalgia for traditional village life has moved some to advocate a reexamination of the rural village and the resurrection of strong communal ties. Yet the social and institutional changes that have taken place suggest that such a restoration is impossible. Just as no one would expect farmers to trade back their tractors for ox-drawn plows, neither is it possible to contemplate the return of the village to its former solidarity. Rather, agriculture must be freed from the rural society of the *buraku*, and groups purely and functionally for agriculture alone should be formed. At the same time, an organization which transcends occupational and strata lines and which responds to the demands and concerns of all residents should be formed to reorganize village life.

The term "community" in the sociological sense, was first defined about sixty years ago by Robert M. MacIver. It gained wide currency after being used as the title of a paper published by the National Life Council in 1969 in which it was further explained by the subtitle, "Restoration of Humanity in the Living Environment." In contemporary usage it suggests the ideal of an independent, individual-oriented, democratic social unit. It seeks a new kind of solidarity among hamlet members to replace the traditional form in which all members were molded into a cooperative group that gave no priority to individual interests or needs. A new brand of solidarity must be sought which recognizes that the hamlet has become a pluralistic society of heterogeneous elements. Agriculture must be separated from its close ties with the village and built into a new, rationalized, cooperative system. Village management must be based on the ideals of sharing financial burdens and benefits fairly. Farming and non-farming residents alike will have to undertake the tasks of improving their environment. The 1975 census shows that village children play in vacant lots (28 percent), on the grounds of temples or shrines (17 percent), in school or city playgrounds (11 percent), and along the roads (6 percent). Only 4 percent of settlements had playgrounds built especially for children. The much sought-after "community" cannot be created as long as the traditional attitude persists that "children can play in the shrine grounds" and "old people can gather at the temple." Facilities for children and senior citizens at the very least must be devised and built by each hamlet.

The new "community" must discard the parochial isolation of the traditional village and build a new kind of local society that is open yet closely knit. The very concept of community calls for a renewed sense of community within the community. If the first kind of village is one which takes special care to provide for the needs of its youth and its elderly, the second type is one where several villages are able to unite in building sports facilities, at least for a given school district. Ways must be found to create a healthy bond between rural and urban society, to develop the new concept of a "rurban" community through close cooperation with local government.

Chapter Four

The Political Structure of the Rural Village

The Prewar Village

Administration and Finance

The institutionalization of local government in Japan began with the enactment of the Local Government Law in 1888. The law provided that villages in existence since the Tokugawa period (the vast majority of which were agricultural hamlets) be amalgamated into larger administrative units during 1889 and 1890, and the history of local government begins at this point.

In 1871, the government had adopted the Family Registration Law, which was implemented in 1872 through the *kochō* system. This system divided each prefecture into districts and sub-districts, the districts administered by a chief and his deputy, and the sub-districts superintended by the *kochō*. All these were officially appointed posts, but in the approximately 80,000 villages and towns within these sub-districts, elections were held in which all property owners were eligible to vote for the deputy *kochō*.

In 1878, three additional sets of regulations for local administration were promulgated: a law for the formation of local districts, towns, and villages, rules for prefectural assemblies, and an ordinance on local taxation. The first of these stipulated that for each village and town a *kochō* be appointed who would carry on the traditional functions of self-government, as well as handle the business of national administration. Under this new law, villages were forced to bear a heavy financial burden, one particularly onerous for those averaging about 100 households.

The burden was particularly heavy in education. In the Tokugawa period, education in the village was conducted mainly in *terakoya*, or temple schools, where only the male children of the ruling strata learned the fundamentals of reading, writing, and arithmetic. In the modern period, as the system of compulsory education became established, the construction and maintenance of schools was naturally too formidable a financial task for small hamlets to handle, and communities had to pool their efforts on the village or wider geographical level. Not only in education but in other areas as well, traditional villages often lacked the power to attain the administrative standards required by the national government. In 1884, in an effort to strengthen that power, a *kochō yakuba* was built for groups of five hamlets of approximately five hundred households and headed by officially appointed *kochō*. But conflicts developed easily between the new *kochō yakuba* and the traditional villages, making it clear that some other form of local administrative system was needed.

The popular rights movement which had arisen throughout the nation from the early Meiji era was eventually suppressed by the government, but the demand for local self-government could not be stifled. In order to prevent a resurgence of the movement, the government set about to establish a system of bureaucratic control over the villages. Before promulgating a constitution and adopting a parliamentary system, the government felt it necessary to create and impose from above new institutions of local self-government and offer local areas what was, at least in form, the power of self-government, thus defeating the growing momentum of the grass-roots movement for local autonomy. However, in substance, the local administration that eventually emerged was under the jurisdiction of the central government and served essentially as the lowest level of national administration under bureaucratic control. In order to shift the administrative burden away from the central government onto local areas, it was necessary to amalgamate existing villages into larger groups, thus augmenting the fiscal base of local government and improving its administrative efficiency.

The institution of the new local government system was begun simultaneously with the amalgamation of the former towns and villages. Amalgamation had actually started at the beginning of the Meiji era, so that in 1889, there were about 71,000 villages and towns in the nation. Further amalgamation reduced the number to about one-fifth, or 39 cities and 15,589 villages and towns. Needless to say, the amalgamation was forcibly carried out on the authority of the central government; it did not reflect any desire on the part of the local people for a new system of local administration. From the point of view of the central government, too, participation in local government was never considered a democratic *right* of local citizens but a duty or obligation to the state.

In this newly formed local government system, however, not all the residents of each district had equal rights. Residents were divided into those who were full-fledged citizens (*kōmin*) and those who were not. Only males over the age of 25 with two years' residence in a given locality, who paid two or more yen in local or direct national taxes, qualified for full citizenship. Only these *kōmin* could vote, and at that time *kōmin* made up only about 10 percent of the entire population. Full citizens were in turn divided into two classes, according to the amount of taxes paid, and all voted for representatives on the village council; but so-called first-class citizens had several times the voting power of the second-class citizens, thereby gaining a firm grip on council elections.

Council members were elected for six-year terms, and half the seats came up for election every three years. Candidates for election, of course, had to be full citizens, and from this group a mayor and his deputy, who served a four-year term, were elected to take charge of administration in the village or town. The mayor also became chairman of the council.

Despite certain shortcomings, the form of local government in the rural village was modern, insofar as village residents could elect a mayor and councilmen. However, this did not permit local autonomy in the true sense of the term, for the village council and the mayor were unable to act independently of prefectural and national government control and supervision. Under the new system the home minister was empowered to dissolve the village or town council, and the mayor and the officials under him could be officially reprimanded or forced to resign by the prefectural governor, who was also appointed by the home minister. The village government offices were less the locus of local autonomy than the last link in the chain of national and prefectural administration.

Thus the local government system begun in 1889 allowed local notables, namely the landlords, to control village administration through limited suffrage and the system of differentiated electoral classes. And, while it appeared in form to permit some local autonomy, in actuality local government was virtually under the full control of the bureaucracy. This centrally directed character of local government persisted, although revisions were made in 1911, 1921, and 1926. Only after World War II was fundamental change finally achieved.

In the 1911 revision, terms for local government councilmen were changed to four years, and elections were to be held every four years; though the powers of the mayor were expanded, central government control was also strengthened. The period after World War I was the heyday of Taishō Democracy, toward the end of which many farmers' unions were organized. The 1921 revision of the local government law was made in order to cope with the burgeoning democratic movement, and it extended suffrage to any male of 25 or over who paid local government taxes. The electorate was expanded, and the system of differentiated electoral classes abolished. The 1926 revision was made in accordance with the adoption of universal manhood suffrage the previous year, and payment of taxes was no longer the criterion for voting eligibility. All of these moves reflect the decline of the power in rural areas of the absentee landlord. The revisions were also designed to prevent class conflict from growing in the villages. But none of these revisions brought real change to local government. It remained under the firm control of the central government. When the nation began to mobilize during the thirties, central government control was even further increased and during the war, local autonomy was practically non-existent.

The financial base of local government in the 1870s and 1880s, which had to support a much greater administrative load than its

Tokugawa predecessor, merits a thorough discussion. Under order of the feudal lord, the Tokugawa village had been required to compile some tax and other records, but as Japan set out to achieve the status of a modern nation-state, the volume of administrative tasks required of the villages by the central government increased immensely. As mentioned before, the new burden was further augmented by the needs of building school facilities, and was by no means lightened by the inauguration of local government in 1889. Quite to the contrary, it was made heavier. Increased funds were required for administrative buildings and functions as part of the political integration effort, and for educational facilities to support the development of a capitalist economy. Despite the greater importance assigned them, the towns and villages were never provided adequate financial resources to carry out their role. In principle, the main source of local funds consisted of revenue from village-owned assets, registration fees, and other handling charges. A supplementary source was a surtax which villages and towns were allowed to collect at a certain percentage of prefectural and national taxes, but the local government was advised by central authorities to avoid collecting taxes of its own, and independent taxing was exceptional. Thus, although the nation had started a local government system, the village was unable to locate any new source of funds. In many instances, the hamlet-owned assets were not transferred to the new administrative village, so funds from public assets were negligible. At the inception of the local government system, revenue from commonly owned assets made up only 3 percent on the national average, leaving villages and towns with only the most meager financial base.

Under the compulsory budget system of local government, villages and towns could not refuse to pay for expenses as ordered by prefectural or national authorities. It was unable to reject the excessive administrative duties delegated to it by prefectural and central government, but had, above all, to find ways to handle those duties with small fiscal resources. Since administrative expenses and education were made obligatory priorities, this naturally meant that projects for the village proper had to be severely cut back. As Table 38 shows, after village or town finances were used for these two major priorities,

Table 38   Trends in Local Public Finance (percent)

Revenue	1882	1891	1906	1921	1930	1945
Local surtax on national taxes	91.5	63.3	61.4	62.2	20.3	15.5
Independent taxes	—	1.8	1.3	1.1	22.5	5.5
Grants and subsidies from central government	—	11.5	5.3	7.1	18.2	40.9
Local government bonds	—	1.4	6.6	3.4	10.2	1.5
Other sources	8.5	22.0	25.4	26.2	28.8	36.6
Total	100.0	100.0	100.0	100.0	100.0	100.0
Expenditures						
Salaries and administrative expenses	17.1	35.6	29.0	27.9	18.5	32.0
Education	35.3	32.7	40.6	44.4	42.6	13.0
Public works	34.2	26.3	8.7	8.8	8.0	10.9
Industry and commerce	0.6	0.5	1.4	1.6	1.8	10.6
Social security	—	—	—	—	2.6	—
Servicing of debts	—	1.0	5.8	1.8	7.0	5.0
Other expenditures	12.8	3.9	14.5	15.5	19.5	28.5
Total	100.0	100.0	100.0	100.0	100.0	100.0

little was left for other needs. A large percentage of funds was directed toward construction, but the bulk of this was used for building the roads and bridges required by national government policy to help shift the country away from a self-sufficient to a modern capitalist economy. It was very difficult to obtain funds from local government for projects directly related to farm production, such as the building of farm roads or irrigation canals, and even if funds were forthcoming the sum was far from adequate. In general, farm projects had to be accomplished through the financial support and uncompensated labor of local residents.

These financial constraints alone illustrate how difficult it was for local government to make decisions or to conduct its administration independently. Such conditions implicitly required that the Tokugawa village be retained in the form of the hamlet. When funds for construction were inadequate, the hamlet was forced to produce the needed amount for roads and irrigation system repair, just as it had in the past. Local government was also afflicted by a shortage of personnel, and, until wartime mobilization began, there were, in addition to the mayor, deputy mayor, and revenue officer, only two or three secretaries to handle administration. Because of the fiscal weakness of local government, the hamlet was used as much as possible as the administrative unit.

As the modern state and the capitalistic economy became established, the demand for efficient administration grew stronger. Heavy military expenditures severely curtailed the government budget for domestic administration; hence the national government forced the town and village governments, by providing them with token subsidies, to carry out many administrative functions on its behalf. The leverage gained by subsidies further weakened what small autonomy had been retained by local government, and the village was further subordinated to national and prefectural policy.

The system of universal national subsidies was instituted following the Great Depression of 1929. And in order to push the rural areas out of their severe economic plight, the government lauched public works construction projects and the rural reconstruction movement. Even these efforts did not achieve economic recovery, however, necessitating massive government subsidies. The development of the munitions industry during the 1930s had widened the economic gap between regions, another reason that national government found creation of a system to subsidize financially disadvantaged areas indispensable. Again, this policy further accelerated the centralization of the control of public finance.

The wartime mobilization completely subordinated local government to central authority. After the rural reconstruction movement began, the hamlet took on added importance as the basic unit of self-help. As the nation prepared itself for a total war, the hamlet association, along with its urban counterpart, the *chōnaikai*, was formally incorporated into the state apparatus. Institutionalized as the bottom-level unit of national administration, the hamlet and the neighborhood associations were placed under the direct supervision and control of the village or town mayor. Local autonomy was struck a fatal blow and state authority finally permeated the entire society.

Until after World War II, the Japanese people did not have local autonomy in the real sense of the term. Controlled by state authority, local government was occupied completely with the jobs assigned from above, barely being able to manage the system of public education. Some autonomous projects were carried on with the scarce funds that remained, but because the villages and towns had to rely so heavily on the hamlet to perform their administrative functions, and because conflicts of interest often broke out between the hamlets, local government was constantly plagued by the lack of unity and creativity.

Administrative Village Government and the Hamlet

The villages set up under the new local government system were charged with a heavy load of administrative work as the lowest echelon of state government, and they did not have the financial resources with which to conduct independent activities of self-government. As a result, the hamlet had to carry on the traditional activities of self-government. In addition, as discussed in Chapter Three, the administrative village passed on many of the tasks both of national and local administration to the hamlet, using it as the most basic unit of public administration.

Nevertheless, at the inception of the new system of local government, the hamlet was only considered a convenient division for administrative coordination. It had been the national government's intention to establish a new system of local government by amalgamating the former *mura* into new administrative villages. Village assets were expected to provide revenue which would cover most of the expenses of local government, on the assumption that those assets could be pooled for that purpose. But when the new system was instituted, almost no hamlet assets were transferred to the jurisdiction of the administrative village. The hamlets clung tenaciously to their assets, and the issue gave rise to hamlet sectionalism. In 1910, the central government attempted to enforce a policy of amalgamation of hamlet assets and to place them under administrative village or town control. The program met stiff resistance from hamlet residents, and even when property was nominally shifted to the local government, in most cases actual control remained with the hamlets. Also, there were many hamlets which divided up ownership of communal property among individuals or placed it under joint registration as a way to thwart this national government effort. The central government also attempted to bring together into one shrine the local guardian deities which were in many senses the symbols of hamlet solidarity, another aspect of the effort to promote the unity of the new administrative village. Yet this campaign was not successful either. The traditional communal order was thus firmly preserved in the hamlet.

While the *buraku* remained strong even in the face of central authority, that very solidarity eventually proved extremely useful to the national government. In general, hamlet unity had weakened as more and more landlords became parasitic and their control lost its grip, but in the wake of the economic devastation and social unrest that had shaken rural Japan in the late twenties, the government undertook a campaign to promote *buraku* unity. Also, as mentioned before, when the nation began to mobilize for war, the government institutionalized the hamlet associations (*burakukai*), making them responsible for the quotas of food supplies required from the hamlets upon which the all-out war effort heavily depended.

Thus, the relationship of the hamlet with the administrative village or town was not consistent under the Meiji local government system which persisted until the end of World War II. But, in any case, the hamlet remained the basic unit of self-government and maintained a strong solidarity, in the face of fundamental weaknesses in administrave village leadership and finance. Local government could do little more than adjust conflicts of interest among its component hamlets. The lack of adequate funds prevented local government from pursuing a positive program of self-government which could transcend *buraku* sectionalism in the village or town as a whole.

In local politics, the hamlets consistently put their own interests before those of the entire village, making the planned, rational allocation of funds to hamlets for production promotion and construction purposes very difficult. This also made it impossible to establish program priorities for each fiscal year. In most instances, all the hamlets sought to gain a share of village funds, and hamlet strength, through its representatives in the local governemnt council, was the decisive factor in obtaining these funds. Concerning the assessment of taxes, which was based on a certain amount per household, the hamlet representatives were expected to push for a decision advantageous to their hamlet. Until explicit regulations were established in 1911 for the assessment of prefectural taxes, the standards were very vague, in part because assessment was still largely based on an arbitrary ranking by family wealth and status. The hamlet representative who was well informed about his constituents and would take a strong stand in their interests was necessary since the main guidelines in tax assessment were a combination of income, assets, and size of family.

The hamlet, therefore, endeavored to send as many representatives to the village council as its voting population would permit. In many instances, elections were not actually held because through prior adjustments the total number of candidates was restricted to the number of seats allocated to each hamlet according to its size. When elections were held, hamlet leaders generally controlled the votes by dividing up the hamlet and instructing the residents of each division to vote for a particular candidate. When a small hamlet did not have enough voters to send its own representative to the council, it would join together with a neighboring hamlet in the support of a designated candidate. At the next election, the favor would be returned by giving combined support to the other hamlet's favorite son. Hamlets that could not control their votes and in which votes went over to candidates from other hamlets were derided with names like kusakariba or magusaba, meaning "open pasture."

The candidate for village-town council representative was almost without exception a powerful local landlord, and frequently he stayed in office for a long time. If someone with influence and authority was not available in the hamlet, it would review all potential candidates and choose one to run on its behalf. When, in the wake of socioeconomic changes, the number of candidates became numerous, hamlets held a kind of primary election to reduce the number in order to guarantee that their administrative village councilmen faithfully represented hamlet interests. When a deal could not be reached on the candidate, an "estimated vote" would be drawn up, taking into account all those who could be depended on to vote for a particular candidate, including tenants. relatives, employees, and neighboring farmers. Votes were sought in other hamlets as well, but the bulk of support came from the candidate's home hamlet. Even in hamlets disrupted by tenancy disputes and the growth of farmers' unions, candidates could count on the votes of their own hamlets.

Not only councilmen but the officers of other village-wide organizations were considered representatives of hamlet interests. Many groups were set up on the administrative village level. The producers' cooperatives (authorized by the 1900 Industrial Cooperative Act), the farm associations (*nōkai*) composed of landlords, and the wartime amalgamation of these two groups, the agricultural associations (*nōgyōkai*), were all examples of such groups. Like the producers' coops, the agricultural organizations were not necessarily formed simultaneously or uniformly throughout the nation, but inevitably had to be created in conformity with government-prescribed rules. Also, while they were not formed on the initiative of local residents, their officers, as in the case of the administrative village council, were selected on the basis of hamlet representation. In turn, these organizations made use of the hamlet and formed sub-units within it.

Mechanisms of Administrative Village and Town Government

The local government system enacted in 1888 was for all intents and purposes landlord government. This is because under the system of limited franchise and differentiated electoral classes it was easy for large landowners to gain seats on the village council, and most of the seats on the council were filled by these landlords who also happened to be *oyakata* and stem family heads. The positions of mayor and deputy mayor, who were selected by the council members, usually went to the most powerful landlords, or to lesser landlords who would follow their lead. In many cases these smaller landlords achieved the position of mayor after having worked their way up from a position in the town administration, such as revenue officer or deputy mayor. They were invariably attentive to the will of the powerful members of the council, to whom they owed their positions.

Thus local government was conducted on the basis of the system of landlord control in the hamlets. The major concern of the council was how to achieve a balance among the hamlets, each of which was a self-contained governing unit. In every major issue, such as how to allocate the meager funds available for civil engineering projects among the hamlets, in what proportions to collect various donations and other funds, and in taxation how to achieve a fair apportionment among the hamlets in the estimation of the amount-per-household for each hamlet, council representatives constantly asserted the interests of their own hamlets. The hamlet's strength stood behind the councilmen, and inter-hamlet power relations determined the conduct of village government.

Naturally, the strength of a hamlet was not determined by its size alone, but by the strength of the hamlet landowners. A councilman's voice in the local government council was dependent on the combined weight of his own holdings and the social and economic strength of his hamlet. Thus, projects decided by the village council and carried out by village administration were consistent not only with the interests of the hamlet, but with those of the landowning strata. When funds could be obtained from the village treasury for road construction or irrigation projects, for example, the hamlet would have to augment those funds with its own money and labor. Such projects were nominally undertaken for the benefit of the entire hamlet, but the advantages were enjoyed most by the landowning strata. The large landlords whose holdings spread over several hamlets benefited in particular from the local government system.

The coincidence of landlord and hamlet interests changed little after landlords became more parasitic. When the system of limited suffrage was abolished and universal manhood suffrage was instituted, the council membership expanded to include owner-cultivators and well-to-do part-owner/part-tenant farmers. Even then, the identification of landlord and hamlet interests persisted. Hamlet interests were foremost in the farmer's mind, and that overriding concern obscured the latent conflict of interest between different strata in the hamlet. The poor tenant farmers at the bottom of the hierarchy were thus blinded to the interests of their own class. While "hamlet interests" appeared to be neutral and transcend the interest of any particular stra-

tum, they were, in the final analysis, the interests of the landlord and the wealthier farmers.

The village council functioned to coordinate the interests of
each hamlet, or more accurately, the interests of the landlords.
When a few powerful landlords on the council exercised strong
leadership in accommodating hamlet interests, village administration went smoothly. Also, if there was a single landlord
powerful enough to control all the hamlets represented in the
village council, government could still be innovative. But when
there was no landlord with such influence, the landlord councilmen representing each hamlet vied with one another and the
village government could barely manage to maintain a workable equilibrium, let alone engage in creative self-government.
In order to conduct innovative village government it was necessary to break the stultifying balance of power created from the
unwillingness of anyone to upset the status quo. After the institution of local government, in villages where inter-landlord rivalry was recurrent and agreement could not be reached, the
mayor's position was insecure and turnover was high. Factional
strife, which flared up in the name of hamlet interests, was
chronic, and village administrations became less and less active.
When, on top of limited finances, representatives persisted in
quibbling over the minor policy points, government was obviously
unable to initiate progressive programs of self-government.

On the whole, prewar village or town government never became strong enough to promote unified, planned programs for
developing the interests of the entire village, and the members
of the village council never acted as representatives for the entire
village rather than their own hamlet constituencies alone. Councilmen considered their positions largely honorary. In order to
become council members, they were never required to have the
vision or capability of reforming village administration; it was
sufficient if they had enough ability to prevent hamlet interests
from being infringed upon. That ability derived from family status based on landownership as well as experience in hamlet or
village government. The councilmen's efforts in government
were respected by the villagers as long as the traditional balance
was not impaired. For the residents of hamlets where the forms
of self-government had been retained from the former Toku-

gawa-period *mura*, it was taken for granted that the hamlet conduct hamlet projects and if the representative succeeded in obtaining even a small sum from village funds, it was applauded. If the amounts which had to be contributed or the expenses that had to be shouldered by the hamlet were not unjust, it was considered the result of the representative's efforts.

Under such conditions, the administrative village council was not a forum for debate on the development of the village. The village councilman's job was simply to adjust conflicting interests among the different hamlets; he was not concerned with carefully weighing and balancing the interests of the different strata in the entire village. Councilmen could perform their functions rather intuitively and without debate because the adjustment of hamlet interests, which obscured the fundamental class conflict, was essentially no more than the coordination of landlords' interests. Most important decisions were made not in the council chambers, but settled beforehand in informal discussions, and the council meeting minutes almost always recorded that there were "no objections."

By the end of the 1920s, however, others began to compete with landlords for control of village government. The interests of the lowest class of tenants were still ignored, but as landlords became increasingly parasitic and part-owner farmers began to participate more in village government, hamlet and landlord interests could no longer be simply set apart. In addition, conflicts between the urban and rural areas of the village increased. The minutes of the village council now began to record traces of dissent and argument. This became even more common especially in villages where farmers' unions were becoming powerful enough to send their own candidates to the council.

These changes, however, were brought to a halt by the shift toward war mobilization in the 1930s. The village became the last link in the chain of organization for the all-out war effort and lost all vestiges of autonomy under the pressures of national administration.

Postwar Change in Village Government

Reform of the Local Government System

Under the pressures and directives of the Allied Occupation, many democratic and institutional reforms were imposed. The new Constitution, promulgated in 1947, contained a chapter on local government not part of its Meiji predecessor, which guaranteed the right of local self-government. Now constitutionally based, Local Government Law was designed to completely refurbish the system of local government.

As previously mentioned, voting rights in the Meiji era were determined by amount of tax paid. The vote was extended to all males in 1925, but the franchise still did not apply to men under 25 nor to women. The first accomplishment of the new Constitution was to guarantee the right to vote to all men and women 20 or over who were residents of a given locality for at least three months, and any man or woman 25 years of age could become a candidate for local office. Second, the new law stipulated that the village council select its own chairman (previously the mayor had served as ex-officio chairman) and that the mayor be directly elected by all the villagers. Third, the voters could now petition for establishment or revocation of ordinances, the audit of any specific accounts, the dissolution of the village council, or the dismissal of the village mayor or particular council members, giving local residents much augmented powers. Fourth, national control of the mayor and of the village council was almost completely eliminated, and the former power of the home minister and the prefectural governor to dissolve the council or dismiss its members was abolished. Legal sanctions on interference in local government were no longer binding, and autonomy was guaranteed by law.

Yet all these institutional reforms were imposed as part of the policy of democratization being pursued by the Occupation. They were not the culmination of spontaneous efforts by local efforts. Subsequently, in the course of Occupation changes in policy, conditions changed considerably. In addition, local government was forced to rely on the central government for financial support so that though national controls were formally abolished, local autonomy was still unrealized.

Local police forces and decentralized educational administration set up on the basis of an elected board of education did not remain viable for long after they were organized. Although established in name, local government was plagued by deficits and could not establish a solid fiscal base. Under the constraint of central government financing, local government in Japan remained, as it had always been, under the effective control of centralized state authority.

The system of local government finance was also thoroughly reformed after the war, but lagged behind the new institutions of self-government. It was not reformed until 1950, three years after the promulgation of the Local Government Law. Under the reform, the administrative village was to collect revenues in the form of a local resident's tax and a tax on immovable property, and this gave the village greater freedom of action than previous methods of collecting revenue. Economically disadvantaged villages, of course, could not conduct effective self-government on these revenues alone. The postwar expansion of compulsory education required that villages build new middle schools, and local finances were such that they were forced to turn to the state treasury for subsidies and equalization grants. Equalization grants were awarded when local revenues did not reach a fixed national standard, but the grants were invariably much too small. Because supplementary funds were always in short supply, the burden was always greatest on the village. Thus, insofar as local governments had to rely to a large extent on national funds, though they might be institutionally autonomous, in reality they were still firmly under the control of state authority.

On the other hand, despite their dependence on central government finance, local fiscal difficulties were not resolved. This was only natural, since after the war the central government's overriding objective was the reconstruction of the capitalist economy on the national level, and little was left over to rescue local governments from their financial plight. The number of village and town governments with deficits increased year by year, until only a few years after the system had been established conditions were so acute that a reamalgamation of local areas could no longer be avoided. This revision made all too obvious the weaknesses of local government not formed by the local residents themselves. In other words, the revisions were not initiated by village people in answer to the felt need for change, but like the Meiji-era amalgamation of villages, were imposed from above. The changes were instituted in the Law for the Promotion of Town and Village Amalgamation of 1953, but as we shall see in the following section, this reform, known as the Shōwa Village Amalgamation, was undertaken less to address the problems of local self-government than to resolve the issue of rationalization of the administrative and financial mechanisms of the state. In other words, it was a central government initiative taken in the effort to minimize grants and subsidies to local government and to ensure efficient utilization of state funds.

Local Administration before the Shōwa Amalgamation

Systemic reforms undertaken after the war produced many substantive changes in village government. The Imperial Rule Assistance Association (IRAA) organized during the war had branches in every village and the village mayor served as the head of the IRAA branch. As a result of the purges following the war, all such mayors were removed from office, and amid the subsequent turmoil, elections for new mayors were held. In many villages, former landlords or others who were little more than stand-ins for the purged mayors were elected to the positions, but among them were also many newcomers and exceptionally able men who had returned to the villages from the cities or from abroad after demobilization. The agricultural land reform had a tremendous impact on the villages, and the changes that ensued profoundly affected mayoral elections. The new mayors were accorded higher status than their predecessors, who had often been no more than mediators in the deliberations of the village council. They now ran for office on special political platforms and were elected on the promise that they would pursue certain policies, so the new mayors took a much more active posture in local administration.

Land reform and the profound changes it brought to the social hierarchy also reflected in the composition of the village council. While the councils had once been made up of landlords and owner-farmers or sometimes part-owners with large holdings, after the war it was not unusual for those who had been tenants before the reform to be elected to council positions. Also, since women were eligible to vote, women council members began to appear, although their numbers remained small. It became rare, moreover, for council members to be elected without a vote, since there were now many candidates competing for office. Election campaigns for mayor and councilman were especially fierce in villages where the farmers' unions had been organized to resist attempts by landlords to thwart the land reform. A democratization movement in the villages touched off by the farmers' unions was gaining momentum in many areas.

In spite of all these changes, however, the mechanisms of local government were still not radically affected. Even after the war, a large percentage of those who held the positions of mayor and village councilman were members of the former landlord strata. According to the 1953 survey of 90 villages and towns throughout the country, 57 percent of the three major village administrative positions and 39 percent of the council seats were held by former landlords (see Table 39). The number of former tenants was very low. Significantly, the basis of electoral support for these offices was still in the hamlet and councilmen continued as before to be hamlet representatives. That aspect of village government had not changed.

Table 39   Holders of Village Offices by Pre–Land Reform Ownership Status, 1953 (percent)

Office	Landlord	Owner-farmer	Part-tenant	Tenant
Mayor, deputy mayor, treasurer	57	20	16	7
Councilman	39	22	28	9

This does not mean, however, that the qualifications for choosing village councilmen had not changed since before the war. While former landlords were numerous among village councilmen, they no longer enjoyed much economic power because the land reform had taken away their power base. It is more reasonable to think that the landlord's former wealth had made it possible to obtain a higher level of education than most farmers, giving him the advantage in elections for village office.

While it is true that landlord power lingered even after the postwar reforms, family status and economic strength were not enough to qualify for election to office; now ability became a crucial factor. The leveling of the upper class brought more candidates up for election, and it became difficult to narrow the field only through informal agreement and adjustment within the hamlet. In most cases, primary elections had to be held. Hamlet control over voting behavior was much curtailed, so that the simple declaration of one's intention to run no longer ensured that he would be voted in; candidates were forced to actively campaign for office. In order to prevent votes from being drained off by candidates from other hamlets, guards would be posted at night to prevent campaigners from stealing in to secure votes for candidates outside. Yet, even when vote control was weak, the number of those voting for non-hamlet candidates was not an appreciable majority. This was true even in villages where farmers' unions organized across hamlet lines struggled against the conservative power of the ex-landlords. Union-sponsored candidates garnered the majority of their votes in their home hamlet.

While hamlet interests remained the ultimate concern of residents, under the new local government system, they were much less amenable to leaving the affairs of their community unquestioningly in the hands of councilmen who were rich farmers or landlords. In turn, villagers began to make greater demands on hamlet representatives. Council members were no longer as free to make convenient compromises at their own whim, and pressure from constituencies made assertion of hamlet interests all the stronger. Recalling the difficulty encountered in continuing the wartime food quota system to help cope with persisting food shortages after the war, it is easy to understand why the changed attitudes among local people made it all the harder. Village government was no longer the distant entity to which farmers surrendered control in deference to the authority of the upper strata. It was now very close at hand, and the interest and concern of the ordinary citizen in the political affairs of his village rose markedly. As a result, administrators who could not demonstrate their ability to act on behalf of local citizens did not stay in office long.

Generally speaking, the prestige of holding an official position of power and authority was not substantially reduced. Though the knowledge spread that anyone could now become a council member regardless of social status, it did not affect the association of prestige and honor with official duty. That alone convinced a candidate that he was working solely for the benefit of his own hamlet.

Despite these many problems, increased interest in local affairs after the war promised a major turnabout in self-government in Japan. If such attitudes had spread, grass roots democracy might have become more than a slogan, but the roots never really took strong hold. For one thing, under the program for expanding the compulsory education system, already meager local funds had to be devoted to building new middle schools and the village did not have the financial resources to actively develop self-government initiatives. For another, when the land reform was completed and the farmers' unions began to break up, the consciousness of strata interests which had nurtured rudimentary democratic thinking gradually disappeared. Limited finances also caused the village to rely on the hamlet for help, and the notion of local government encompassing the entire village or town did not develop.

The Hamlet and Village Consolidation

After the initial amalgamation of the *mura* under the Meiji system of local government, some further mergers were made. The first amalgamation reduced the number of villages and towns to about 16,000, and by the end of the war the number was just a little more than 11,000. About 4,000 villages and towns were not only merged but simply absorbed into expanding urban areas. Most villages and towns, however, continued to function as self-governing units.

Several financially difficult years in the new postwar village system led to the large-scale amalgamation of 1953, the most massive since the 1889 adoption of local government. The government promoted the 1953 town and village amalgamation law on the promises that amalgamation would 1) strengthen the fiscal base of local government, 2) hold down expenditures and increase capital outlays, 3) provide a broader base for the recruitment of village officials, 4) rationalize personnel organization, thus increasing efficiency, and 5) raise the level of local welfare programs and provide better public facilities.

Just as the Meiji amalgamation was initiated by the central government to create a strong financial base for local government and improve its administrative capabilities, the Shōwa amalgamation was intended to upgrade the efficiency of national administration and free the central government of the burden of local government deficits. The promise to improve public welfare was little more than an attractive slogan. The policy was, in effect, a device to gloss over contradictions inherent in centralized public finance, and to keep local government as cheap as possible.

Similarly, although the post–World War II amalgamation was not applied to all villages by fiat as was the case during the Meiji era, both national and prefectural governments promoted it with enthusiasm and provided a form of authoritarian direction. To promote amalgamation, the central authorities promised that any village that amalgamated within three years would receive an assortment of benefits. The local people, on their part, fell for these offers without contemplating the long-range ramifications of the merger for self-government. Popular concern for local autonomy was minimal, allowing influential local leaders to monopolize negotiations for amalgamation as carried out on the advice of prefectural authorities. Exactly which villages and towns would merge was often decided in consideration of the personal interests of those leaders. In a number of cases the merging partners were not the most appropriate. Some villages decided to become part of a nearby city partly because the words "city resident" had a better ring than "village resident" and "city councilman" sounded better than "village councilman."

The Shōwa amalgamation seems to have been conducted less dictatorially than its Meiji predecessor, judging from the large number of disputes that ensued in the villages and complaints

about the way amalgamation had been conducted. These disputes often arose when preliminary discussions had been inadequate, prompting hamlets to oppose the amalgamation. When
such conflict disrupted hamlet unity, the antagonism that followed was extraordinarily bitter. The rational solution would
have been to split such hamlets and merge each side with units
that served its interests best, but that was only a last resort. Pre-
dictably, the old administrative villages and towns were destined
to become, under the new local government system, the basic
units of solidarity that the hamlet had been under the Meiji
system. In other words, a sense of town or village solidarity has
been fostered ever since the Meiji reforms which resisted division and cemented the hamlets in the village into a unified body.

In all cases, amalgamation resulted in larger villages and
towns. The standard was originally set at an average population
of about 8,000 each, but in fact they were much larger. The
law went into effect in October 1953 and had been carried out
throughout most of the nation by September 1956. In those three
years the number of local government units was reduced by
6,000, to about one-third the previous number (see Table 40.)

Table 40   Change in Number of Cities, Towns, and Villages

Year	City	Town	Village	Total
1930	99	1,528	10,292	11,919
1940	125	1,706	9,614	11,445
1950	235	1,862	8,346	10,443
1953	286	1,976	7,606	9,828
1957	501	1,920	1,365	3,786
1960	555	1,930	1,023	3,508
1970	595	2,000	673	3,268
1975	643	1,974	640	3,257

The number of villages formed in purely farming areas sharply
declined and the number of cities doubled, for many villages
were absorbed into cities. No longer could one speak of rural
self-government solely in terms of the administrative village or
town, for vast rural areas now encompassed by the cities have to
be taken into consideration.

How did the hamlet change after amalgamation? Under the
old village system, most hamlets except the smallest had been

able to send at least one representative to the village council. But under the new municipality, one town or village council member is allowed only for several hamlets. In the old system, small hamlets often joined together to elect the candidate of their choice, but in the new, even when several hamlets cooperate, there is no assurance that their chosen candidate will be elected, for the number of votes required is now much greater and hamlet control over voting behavior is weaker. The old attitudes prevail, nonetheless, and hamlet members continue to support council candidates who represent their own and adjacent hamlet interests or those of the Meiji administrative village. Since the councilman must, in any case, represent a much wider area than the hamlet, individual hamlets have no one to speak up for their interests in the council. Thus the *buraku*, which had long played the leading role in rural politics, was forced into the background and found it necessary to ally itself with other hamlets even to gain seats on the council. This alone represents one of the biggest changes that took place in rural Japanese politics.

One aspect remains the same, however; the hamlet is still an important basic unit in municipal administration. The express purpose of village amalgamation was to strengthen the financial base of local government, but the net result was simply to increase the physical size of that base. It did not succeed in improving the situation so that the *buraku* would no longer have to be relied upon as the lowest administrative unit. Municipal governments newly created through amalgamation tended to make rash promises to the former villages, but they were not financially prepared to fulfill those promises. Even when amalgamation created large village government units, the hamlet still had to supply the funds needed for its own social welfare activities. It apparently occurred to no one that the new administrative unit should take over the major portion of the financial burden borne by the hamlet.

Not only that, the amalgamation greatly expanded the size o administrative districts to cover areas far distant from the municipal office, a factor which also required that the traditional governing functions of the *buraku* be maintained. After amalgamation, municipal offices continued to use the offices of their predecessors as branches or adjunct offices. However, the branches were used only for registrations and tax collection, but local residents resisted giving up the use of such facilities and continued to use them as adjuncts of the main municipal offices. In many cases, these branch or adjunct offices were closed to save money.

Thus the hamlet continued to be used as the basic and most convenient unit of government. Most hamlets still serve as the channel of administrative communication, an inexpensive tool for the collection of taxes, the basic unit for collecting donations for community funds or projects, and the instrument for many other administrative activities, including sanitation and hygiene. Although the village or town supposedly handles all construction expenses, often much of the burden is handed over to the hamlet, which takes care of the jobs with its own cash and labor service.

All these factors continue to sustain and strengthen the hamlet, even though the hamlet is in a state of decline. As long as it is used by municipal administration and as long as it remains no more than a geographical unit within the village, the political structure will retain the principle that local interest comes first and class interests will contine to be obscured by that overriding concern. This point in particicular calls for further study on the new municipal system of self-government.

Farm Village and Local Government Today

Power Structure of Cities, Towns, and Villages

Most rural hamlets before the 1953 amalgamation fell under the jurisdiction of either town or village administration. Since most residents were farmers, local politics revolved around agricultural issues. But amalgamation brought dramatic change; many farm hamlets and villages came within city limits, and the population of villages and towns, which had previously accounted for 63 percent of the nation's total, fell to 45 percent in the statistics. These figures do not mean that the farm population was moving into urban areas, but simply that the rural villages were being swallowed up by the cities.

Thus, when discussing the government and politics of the contemporary farm village, one must also consider the cities, particularly the newly formed cities of the post-amalgamation period. The areas which still retain village status administratively usually have a population of up to 5,000 and most are in mountain or foothill regions. Since commerce and industry are undeveloped in those regions, the political structure changed relatively little after amalgamation. The biggest change is a dramatic decline in the number of administrative villages. Meanwhile, however, the total number of towns in the nation did not decline; even though many became cities by amalgamation, equally many new towns were created through mergers of several villages. In those towns there are usually at least one or two settlements with significant commerce or industry. The political and governmental structure of rural Japan is today strongly affected, not only by agriculture, but by the presence of commerce and industry, and by relations between farming and non-farming districts within a single administrative district.

Another point important to note is the decline in the number of village or town councilmen after amalgamation. As a rule, that number is determined according to population. For example, if five villages, each with a population of 3,000, were merged to become one large town, the combined population would be 15,000. Before amalgamation, each village would have had 16 councilmen, making a grand total of 80. The amalgamation reduced the number to 26, the maximum a town of 15,000 is allowed to have. Also, whereas before, 80 percent of the councilmen would have represented farmers, that figure fell to below 70 percent. Table 41 gives the results of a survey of municipal council elections made while the process of amalgamation was going on. The number of representatives who listed farming as their occupation declined, a trend especially marked in the cities. And since councilmen with ties to commerce and industry usually have greater influence than those representing farming, the effects on local government of reduced village representation in a city or town is proportionately greater. In the more than 200 new cities created through amalgamation, agricultural interests have had particular difficulty gaining fair attention in local politics.

Table 41 Councilmen by Occupation before and after Amalgamations, 1955 (percent)

New Administrative Unit (number in sample)	In Same Area before Amalgamations		In New Units	
	Farmers, Foresters, Fishermen	Other	Farmers, Foresters, Fishermen	Other
Cities (314)	67.1	32.9	45.3	54.7
Towns (914)	75.3	24.7	70.1	29.7
Villages (341)	87.4	12.6	84.9	15.1
Total (1,569)	74.2	25.8	67.5	32.5

Non-farmer delegates to the new municipal council are often small manufacturers or shopkeepers, with a smattering of building contractors and lumber mill operators. The latter usually reside in major towns, but are influential in farming districts because they offer outside employment to part-time farmers. The chambers of commerce organized by non-farming councilmen work at cross purposes to the Nōkyō and attempt to divert the flow of special financial assistance from going to agriculture. Where there is a fairly large factory in a town, factory owners exert much energy toward obtaining funds for areas of their own concern. The factory backs its own employees as candidates in municipal council elections and makes every effort to thwart the allocation of funds to agriculture. Prior to amalgamation, most village funds for industrial and economic activities went into agriculture. The tradition persists on the pretext of protection for the much-reduced and weakened agricultural industry. Government agricultural subsidies are such that local government is forced to provide considerable matching funds, and this means that even today a large portion of local government funds goes to farming projects. Yet while expenditures for commerce and industry are increasing, those for agriculture have generally leveled off. Following the amalgamation, on the whole, local government has tended to give low priority to agricultural affairs, a trend more marked in city than village and town government. Table 42 shows the proportion of city and village/town expenditures devoted to agriculture, forestry, and fishery projects, calculated at the end of fiscal year 1974. Funding by cities

Table 42   Expenditures for Agriculture, Forestry, and Fisheries by Size of Municipality, 1974 (unit = ¥100 million)

	Total Expenditures (A)	Expenditures for Agriculture, Forestry, and Fisheries (B)	B/A
Metropolitan Area	25,336	167	0.7%
City	55,701	2,205	4.0
Town and Village	29,532	3,982	13.5
Total Expenditure	111,680	6,371	5.7

in this area is far too small, at least in comparison with that provided by village/town governments, and this difference is magnified in the case of farm villages which fall within city limits.

The position of mayor, who heads the municipal administration, is now usually filled by a person from an occupation other than farming. Even among village/town mayors, few are farmers by profession. The figures in Table 43 show that in 1959 almost half of all village or town mayors listed their occupation as farming, fishing, or forestry, and since farming claims more of the population than the other two categories, we can assume that most of those mayors were farmers. By the 1970s a little more than one-third of all mayors listed themselves as farmers, which represents a major change from the period when even village mayors who were non-cultivating landlords listed their occupation as farming. The dominance of non-farming mayors is most pronounced in the cities. The easy familiarity between citizens

Table 43   Occupations of Mayors Returned in Nationwide Local Elections (percent)

	Year	Agriculture, Forestry, and Fishing	Commerce	Manufacturing and Mining	Self-Employed	Other	Unemployed
Village and Town Mayors	1959	50.0	8.5	2.6	10.4	18.9	9.6
	1971	35.3	5.7	1.5	24.5	26.9	6.1
	1975	36.4	3.8	1.2	14.0	39.2	5.4
City Mayors	1971	9.9	5.0	—	25.7	53.4	6.0
	1975	7.3	3.7	—	23.5	52.9	12.6

and their mayor has all but disappeared. Whereas people could once make requests directly to the mayor, now, particularly in city and town administrations, the villagers must observe formal procedure, channeling their petitions through a representative who carries the problem to the mayor.

City and village/town administrative offices have been enlarged since amalgamation, and the number of civil servants has increased. Although it was expected that the amalgamation would mean fewer public servants, in fact, the proliferation of administrative work has had just the opposite effect. The organization of municipal offices has been rationalized, and departments have been created with clearly delineated responsibilities and prerogatives. The old village offices had specific divisions too, but work was never approached systematically. It was less efficient than today's administration, but the officials and residents in the old village knew each other on sight and relations were much friendlier and more informal. Once people dropped in spontaneously to the village office to talk over village affairs while sipping tea companionably with officials. That has now been replaced by the impersonal city office, where officers are isolated in separate divisions and cut off from the people they are serving. For better or worse, the friendly village office has become a cold, bureaucratic city hall.

The character of rural councilmen has changed too. Post-amalgamation councilmen must represent constituencies in several hamlets in order to be elected. Control over voting behavior is much more difficult than in the time when each hamlet could run one or more candidates for council office. Candidates need the support not only of their home hamlets but of agricultural groups such as Nōkyō and forestry cooperatives whose membership reaches across the entire area of the former administrative village or town. A candidate must be known over a much wider area and command greater political power than the pre-amalgamation village councilman. His main constituency, however, is still his own and adjacent hamlets, and if elected he is considered a representative of those hamlets, or at most the former administrative village or town in which his hamlet is located. Often the candidate runs as a recommended candidate of his own and neighboring hamlets. As I have shown in Table 44, now few farm-

Table 44   Opinions on Hamlet Recommendation of Candidates (percent)

	Akita		Okayama	
	1953	1968	1953	1968
Of course necessary, because it has always been that way	55.6	6.2	70.3	11.1
Free voting disrupts hamlet harmony	2.2	4.5	5.1	5.2
Good, because it benefits the hamlet	8.4	32.5	7.7	43.8
Prefer free voting	21.5	52.0	10.6	31.6
No opinion	1.9	1.2	1.5	4.5
Don't know	10.4	3.6	4.8	3.8

ers support a candidate solely on the basis of hamlet recommendation, and independent voting behavior is much stronger, yet many voters still support a hamlet-recommended candidate because they believe it is in the best interests of the community. Even among the supporters of free elections, many vote for a candidate because he will defend hamlet interests, so the majority of candidates most likely think of themselves as representing hamlet or local districts, and after being elected they do their best to fulfill those expectations. That councilmen are first and foremost representatives of the interests of the areas which recommended them is still a deeply rooted attitude among farming village voters and the candidates they vote for.

Councilmen elected from an agricultural district feel they must protect the interests of the farming district against those of urban areas and play a part in the development of agriculture. But they are above all conscious of their responsibility to defend the interests of the district, and their main objective is to see that their constituencies get no fewer advantages than other villages. Their priorities must be chosen not only with the interests of agriculture in mind, but with those of the whole district or village region. It is unlikely that representatives from different districts will unite to oppose urban councilmen on behalf of long-range agricultural development. That is why, if they foresee that voters will not protest about building a new city hall or other such project, councilmen think nothing of spending lavishly on it, even if it means borrowing from the national treasury. Indeed, the most visible symbol of village amalgamation is the appearance of splendid new city hall buildings.

The councilmen, therefore, must function as intermediaries between the mayor and his bureaucratic apparatus on the one hand, and the hamlet residents on the other. Relaying their wishes through the hamlet's district chief, the farmers turn to their city or town councilmen to elicit the maximum possible funds from the municipality. If the hamlet receives the desired amount, the success is attributed to the efforts of the council representative. Hamlet leaders may also ask the councilmen to help appeal to the villagers to contribute matching funds for subsidized projects, or to cooperate in getting the project accomplished. Successful mediation in such activities can elevate a councilman to the position of boss of a local district.

In the government of the new municipalities, priority goes to district-wide interests, or those of the former village rather than to strata or occupational interests, and local politics retain much the same logic as during the pre-amalgamation period. As a result of the political needs of this situation, the local district bosses generally support the conservative Liberal Democratic party. Aside from the cities, 90 percent of town and village councilmen claim independent political affiliation, but in fact they are connected with the conservative party, which has been in power almost continuously since 1946. Municipal councilmen do not usually make demands based on explicit strata or occupational interests at council meetings, but they petition for district interests and try to obtain government aid through connections with conservative politicians at prefectural and national levels. About two-thirds of municipal revenue generally comes from independent sources and the remaining third from the national government, a degree of financial dependence which strengthens the ties between local and upper-level echelons of government. Since as much as one-third of local financing comes from the national government, local government is not free even to use the other two-thirds independently—a state known as *sanwari jichi*, or "30 percent self-government." And even that slice of autonomy is controlled by a chain of conservative representatives from municipal councilman and mayor to prefectural assembly and national diet representative.

Change and Stagnation in Municipal Government

The post-amalgamation years have seen numerous constructive developments in local government that would have been impossible under the former system. First, hamlet control over voting has grown steadily weaker, and relatively young candidates who have gained experience and skills through activities in the *seinendan* have been able to compete successfully in elections with the backing of the younger strata of rural society. These younger men are relatively free from binding obligations to their home district and able to act more independently, offering fresh perspectives in politics. They tend to be more reform-minded than the conservative bosses.

Secondly, as a result of amalgamation, in cities and towns with some degree of organized labor, councils tend to include members of reformist and progressive persuasions. Labor union representatives are still a minority, and though they never gave much attention to local government in the past, now they are building an organization to reach workers in outlying districts and becoming more politically involved in areas where the members live. In "bed towns" from which large numbers of workers commute, residents have formed pressure groups, such as the Workers' Council and the Salaried Employees' Union, to resist the heavy tax burden they bear and the disproportionately small benefits they gain from local government. These groups are an effective counterforce to regionalism and the tendency to put local interests before all others. The expanded administrative organization and a greater number of employees in municipal offices after the amalgamation have brought more widespread unionization of local government employees. Today most of them belong to the All-Japan Prefectural and Municipal Workers' Union, a pattern hardly imaginable in the small village of the past.

If these two tendencies, more young reform-oriented candidates in rural politics and increased participation by organized labor, could be skillfully brought together, a new cooperative effort in local government between farmers and urban workers might emerge. Although highly unlikely, if such a coalescence of powers did occur, it could proceed only on very precarious ground. A coalition of farmers and workers is a familial slogan of left-wing dogmatism, but in actuality, such efforts have rarely been successful. Even in cases where a particular incident or problem brings farmers and labor together over some cause, such alliances usually fall apart after a time. Today, citizens' movements are appearing to press for anti-pollution and other measures for the improvement of environmental, social, and economic well-being. But it is not likely that such movements will lead to an effective farmer-labor alliance and bring about reform in local government.

The most important reason for this is that it is difficult for new leadership to emerge among farmers. After amalgamation, as we have seen, a new brand of council representative appeared, but most have fallen into the mold of the old-style village boss. The newly emerging leaders among farmers are in general involved in and committed to agriculture. When they are trying to promote cooperative projects to develop agriculture, they rarely have extra time to engage in municipal politics. The out-of-farm migration of young people in recent years has also weakened the youth groups which once served as the leadership training ground for young people. In addition, potential leaders are drawn off by the lure of urban living and employment, and the drainage of persons of caliber from rural areas is the gravest problem. Among those who still aspire to enter local government, if they have political ambition, the tendency is strong to fall under the sway of the conservative bosses. Even if a person enters politics for the purest of motives and becomes a councilman, he finds few like-minded colleagues. Because he faces the immense task of changing the status quo practically alone, he invariably gives up and gradually becomes more and more like the old-fashioned conservative council member. Even councilmen who seek to bring the fresh air of reform to government and forge an alliance between farmer and labor are soon defeated by the huge gap in interests between agriculture and labor.

A second important reason for the failure of farmer-labor cooperation is that labor itself remains, on the whole, unconcerned with local government. Workers who commute to jobs outside the farm village are concerned about their high taxes, but their dissatisfaction is never transformed into the kind of action that could substantially change local government. The salaried worker is often frustrated because there is no way to conceal how much he earns. His company automatically computes and deducts his taxes, and his income is well known to the tax office. By contrast, the farmer appears fortunate to bear a much lighter tax burden, and the worker often reacts with resentment. The part-time farmer/part-time worker has the advantage of much lighter expenses for food, but his attitude is neither that of a farmer nor of a worker. He is likely to be satisfied with the status quo and in general apathetic about the affairs of local government. The position of the day laborer is the most unstable; he has no union to back him, so he often sides with the construction contractor or the lumber mill operator who employs him. When factories owned by a large corporation are located in a particular locality and employees are serving on the municipal council, their first priority is to protect and promote the interests of their company. The relatively higher standard of living of employees in these corporations places them among the laboring elite in the area, and it rarely occurs to them to help farmers in the municipality or to support the development of agriculture. Employees of subcontractors to the giant companies receive much lower wages, and since their companies have only small numbers of workers, they tend not to go against their employers.

Contemporary local government has changed in various ways, but councils are still controlled by traditional-type bosses elected to office by both urban and rural constituencies, and rural districts are in a much weaker position vis-à-vis urban districts. In an election there is always the danger that the rural representative will lose votes in his stronghold to candidates from urban areas. To guard against this, the candidate invests heavily in the election campaign. Candidates campaign in their local areas in automobiles fitted with loudspeakers, a technique that would have been inconceivable before the war because of the high cost. Now it is commonly used not only by national dietmen but by both city and village council aspirants. The cost is another important factor that deters competent young people from running for office. Even though the ratio of candidates to seats averages only 1.3 to 1, fierce campaigning brings out 90 percent of the voters. Still, the high turnout is less an indication of healthy democratic convictions and concern for local government than of the candidate's ability to attract votes and appeal to residents' deep-rooted loyalty to their local area.

Local Government and Economic Growth

The village amalgamation was carried out when the postwar Japanese economy was still in the process of recovery. Local governments in general suffered financially and many villages were operating on deficits. Amalgamation was designed partially to strengthen the economic base of local government, but even after the reform, the financial situation improved in only a few villages. Financial resources did become more plentiful, but so did the demands for funds. Cities and towns that actively supported amalgamation often made grandiose promises in order to entice neighboring villages and towns into the new groupings, and even when amalgamation involved municipal units that were almost equal in power, plans and promises were often unrealistic. Consequently, many cities, towns, and villages, despite amalgamation, were not only unable to wipe out their deficits, but found them larger than before. In some municipalities where the national government moved in to assist, local government was more restricted than before because it had to cut back on many programs and projects and make greater efforts in tax collection.

As Japan's economy moved into the period of rapid growth, almost every municipality set its sights on higher tax revenues. The national policy of rapid economic growth was based on accelerated development of new industry, and accordingly, municipalities sought to promote the building of factories in their areas. Cities and towns with some financial leeway, in which large factories were situated and which benefited from immovable property taxes, had always been the envy of less fortunate areas. The new growth policy now offered municipalities the chance to gain the means of obtaining such revenues themselves. Some villages knew there was almost no chance of success from the outset, but most others devised plans to induce factories into their area. Location of factories in the area became the cure-all with which local governments expected to extricate themselves from chronic financial distress.

Town and city mayors and influential urban councilmen sincerely believed that industrialization would lead to greater tax revenues, a stronger financial base, and eventually benefits for every citizen. They decided that the investment of meager resources in small industry or farming would never produce the desired tax revenues. Instead they should endeavor to bring industry into the area, eventually to benefit the town through tax revenues. Expenditures for agriculture might have to be cut until the higher tax revenues started to take effect, and the construction of facilities for the welfare of local residents might have to be put aside, but tax funds should be invested in order to build a powerful fiscal resource for the future. This was the logic used by influential town and city leaders concerning local development. Improved welfare for local citizens had been one of the slogans of village amalgamation, but such promises had to be put aside until some future time. In their place appeared the call to bring in industry, the new promise of more effective returns on local investment.

Towns and cities competed to provide the best facilities and local conditions to lure factories. Many municipalities stretched their resources to the limit so that they could offer exemptions or reductions in corporate and property taxes to prospective entries, prepare factory sites, and build roads and water facilities. The trend was most vigorous around 1960 as the entire nation swung into the period of rapid growth. In 1963, when new industrial cities were designated, qualified municipalities engaged in fierce competition. The very intensity of their struggle testifies to the strength of the conviction that prosperity for municipal government was ultimately linked to industrialization. The campaigns to promote industrial investment in this period proved to be among the most intensive ever seen in any country.

The dream, however, was no more than an illusion for most towns. For no matter what incentives a village might offer, companies could reject locations if they were not considered suitable. Even if a town did succeed in seeing a corporation build a factory there, the celebration of the new wealth it promised to bring was inevitably marred by the smoke and waste that the factory brought to the community. The revenue of those cities and towns where factories were built did, in fact, increase, and their financial base did grow firmer. But as revenues rose, national government aid fell proportionately, while local payment for damage and disaster compensation as well as expenses to support anti-pollution and environmental protection measures increased. Promises to improve welfare programs for residents still could not be fulfilled. As the urbanization that accompanies industry brought new needs for more funds, the municipality found it impossible to make plans to promote agricultural production or ease conditions in the farm village.

Despite all the problems, the dream of prosperity through industry was never abandoned by local government leaders. As the growth of the Japanese economy continued to surge ahead, environmental hazards proliferated, and the lessons of pollution became all too clear. As a result, areas that either had no industry or sought more factories refused to consider polluting industries. The burgeoning citizens' movements opposed the introduction of more factories, taking the evils of pollution as their cause célèbre, and local government leaders realized that polluting industries should be informed that they were unwelcome in their constituencies. The extravagant promises that damage compensation would be handled by local government if industry would but build factories there, evaporated. Yet the desire for the benefits of industry remained all the same.

Preoccupied with industrialization, few municipalities have devised solid plans for agricultural improvement and made serious attempts to carry them out. Some municipalities pushed projects to improve the structure of agriculture, as will be discussed later, but most did so simply because they were funded by national government aid. Almost no local government seriously backed or invested in agricultural improvement. Villages that lacked adequate conditions for factories had no choice but to invest in agriculture, so that there are areas that have made major efforts in farming. But most of those villages are poor and have a weak financial base. Isolated mountain villages are almost totally ignored by their municipalities. In the last decade many of these mountain hamlets have turned into veritable "ghost villages" as residents gradually drift away, unable to sustain a livelihood in remote, undeveloped areas. Aid from the administrative village rarely goes to certain communities, even when their very existence is threatened.

Since the 1966 interim report by the Regional Affairs Committee of the Council on Economic Policy, the word *kaso*, or depopulation, has become widely used, and the situation it describes has grown worse. If conditions in the remote areas are such that people from cities can spend their holidays there, the local government will invest in the development of tourist facilities, and in recent years, villages and towns which have found new hope for survival in the tourist industry have proliferated. Many villages were long exploited by profiteering tourist corporations, but in recent years, as the number of short- and long-term visitors has risen, investment by village governments in tourism and summer residence sites has increased. It is better that public rather than private capital be invested in these ventures, but here again, the ulterior motive of local governments is to gain better returns on their investments, and the promise of citizen welfare is still to be fulfilled.

Except for areas potentially suitable for livestock or fruit production, most municipal governments no longer have any solid agricultural policy. Actually, agriculture changed so radically during the period of rapid economic growth that local governments are all but confused about the importance of agriculture in their administration. Especially after 1970, the huge surplus of Japan's most stable product, rice, became a major issue. The government was forced to restrict the acreage planted to this traditionally pivotal crop. Considerable difficulties have ensued, due in large part to inconsistencies in policies of the national government, which has failed to devise a workable agricultural program. Local government and the farmers themselves are also responsible for the problems surrounding surplus rice cultivation.

We should also mention Nōkyō, the agricultural cooperative. It has enormous influence on local government, and even in areas where agriculture does not play a vital role, it is charged with upholding the principle of "farmers united in autonomy, independence, and mutual assistance." But all too often Nōkyō fails to undertake the necessary tasks, even when the absence of

Table 45   Distribution of General Nōkyō by Area Covered (percent)

	1961	1977
Two prefectures or more	0.0	0.1
One prefecture or less	1.0	4.2
County or city	1.7	10.4
Smaller than county	32.3	29.1
Town or village	13.3	34.9
Smaller than town or village	51.7	21.4
Total number of Nōkyō	12,050	4,763

firm and constructive policy prevents the local administration from acting. Apart from specialized crop cooperatives, Nōkyō is the successor of earlier agricultural associations, and its members are drawn from the pre-amalgamation village. For a time after amalgamation, unions tended to remain small. For the most part they performed the functions that had been handled by the old village office. As economic growth accelerated, the numerous small unions found it difficult to keep up, and under the Law for the Promotion of Agricultural Cooperative Amalgamation of 1961 many of them were consolidated. Whereas Nōkyō groups came to about 12,000 at the time the law was passed, fifteen years later consolidation reduced that figure to 4,800. As shown in Tables 45 and 46, consolidation created a few very large Nōkyō groups that encompass areas larger than a city or country district, but 21.4 percent cover less than an entire village district and 32.6 percent have certified membership of less than 500 families, meaning that the total number of consolidated Nōkyō groups is greater than the number of municipalities.

Since small farm cooperatives do not have a strong enough base to respond to the demands of their members, consolidation

Table 46   Distribution of General Nōkyō by Number of Regular Member Households (percent)

Year	≤500	≤999	≤1,999	≤2,999	≤4,999	≥5,000	Average Household No. per Cooperative
1961	63.2	32.1	4.3		0.4		471
1977	32.6	29.5	22.1	8.3	5.5	2.0	1,184

is desirable, but if they are too large, the organization becomes too distant from its members and fails to fulfill its basic mission as a cooperative union. The rise in associate, or non-farming, membership has caused departments in Nōkyō not directly related to farming to expand—areas such as credit services, savings and pension programs, and bulk purchase of consumer goods. Nōkyō activities are more varied and the number of regular employees it hires has greatly increased, but there has been no concomitant increase in the farm operations advisory staff. Only a few farm cooperatives give priority to the very central mission of Nōkyō, the promotion of agricultural development.

Because Nōkyō activities have moved progressively away from the problems of agriculture per se, its political efforts have become basically passive, tending to concentrate on getting higher prices for the rice which the government purchases from farmers. As a pressure group, Nōkyō has taken no initiative in formulating positive programs for agricultural development. Most Nōkyō officials, like municipal mayors and councilmen, tend to be supporters of the conservative LDP and of the status quo. Nōkyō is essentially an economic organization, but it has become an important link in the chain of conservative Japanese politics.

Chapter Five

National Politics and the Village

National Politics and the Farmer

Prewar National Government

Before World War II, the landlords were the only members of the farm village who effectively participated in national politics. According to the Meiji Constitution, sovereignty did not reside in the people, and the ordinary farmer was the passive subject of authority. When parliamentary government was introduced to Japan, voting rights were enjoyed in the rural areas only by landlords and owner farmers; the tenant farmers below them were not permitted to participate. When suffrage was later extended, farmers were still unable to vote for the candidate of their own choice because of the informal control exercised by the hamlet. Voting for seats in the House of Peers set aside for representatives of the highest taxpayers was limited only to very large landlords.

Village and town administration under the local government system of 1889 was essentially government by landlords, so naturally the large landholders were a major force in the national parliament established the following year. During the subsequent two decades Japan barely managed to establish industrial capitalism, and landlords still held about equal leverage in national affairs with the capitalists. A number of landlords, in fact, rose from positions on the county councils or prefectural assemblies to gain seats in the Imperial Diet.

But the capitalist economy began to develop rapidly around the time of World War I, and the political strength of the capitalists grew, while that of the landlord class began to decline. Modern Japan sought to create a "wealthy nation and a strong army," and in this endeavor, agriculture was eventually forced to take second place to the overwhelming priority of building a powerful industrial state. Needless to say, the interests of capitalists were put before those of landlords. In the late 1920s, following the rapid increase of tenancy disputes, a number of programs were adopted, including support for owner-cultivators and regulation of land rents, both measures which reflect the declining priority of landlord interests. Then during the war, as part of food supply quotas assigned to the villages, landlords had to give up the rice in their storehouses for the war effort, a further step in the erosion of their fortunes. The land reform initiated by the Japanese government after the war to redistribute agricultural lands was designed to secure a steady food supply for the reconstruction of the capitalist economy at the expense of landlord interests. This is a clear indication that by that time the landlords no longer carried much weight in national politics.

The relative importance of the landlords in national politics waned rapidly during the early decades of this century, but their position of political leadership in the villages was sustained, though gradually weakening, until the land reform. From the first parliament in 1890 when the landlords first entered national politics until the mid-1920s, their own financial assets were sufficient to provide plentiful funds for political activities. These self-backed, independent politicians from rural areas were known as *idobei* dietmen, who might, at the end of their careers, be impoverished to the point of owning little more than a well and the wall around their property. Later, the *zaibatsu* became the contributors of political funds, and this was a major issue in the conflict between the two leading political parties, the Seiyūkai and the Minseitō. While the composition of the Imperial Diet was gradually changing, the farmers continued to support candidates backed by local landlords. The landlords, by virtue of their control over rural votes, were the most important stratum with whom the dietman had to maintain close ties.

During the first 25 years of parliamentary politics in Japan, the large landlords who were Diet representatives had a strong electoral base built on close relations with other landlords in their constituency. Because suffrage was limited to certain privileged groups, the structure of the political base, built largely on personal and business connections, was relatively simple. Even when suffrage was extended, a candidate could be almost certain of popular votes if he had the support of the landlord and his influential associates. When landlords in the same village were split between different candidates, the rivalries of national politics were often played out on the local level. Competition between the two national parties often divided landlords along party lines and the repercussions of the split were inevitably felt in village politics. Even so, national and local politics were not necessarily closely intertwined, nor did the farmers necessarily have an abiding interest in politics on the national level. Both parties were conservative, and there was no great difference in their policies. Conflicts which arose were mainly those involving personal connections rather than policy. In national elections farmers invariably voted not out of political involvement but as an expression of personal loyalty to an individual landlord.

In villages where farmers' unions were active and well-organized under a central body, some farmers, although a minority, broke away from the mechanical pattern of voting for the landlord-backed candidate and supported people of their own choice from the proletarian parties. These farmers rejected the attitude that both landlord and candidate, simply by virtue of the status accorded them by the village hierarchy, merited unquestioning loyalty and support. But proletarian parties remained an insignificant force in national politics, never posing any real threat to control by the political magnates. Farmer support for those parties is significant for its ideological implications, but it constituted only a small portion of the total farm vote.

The development of party politics was cut short by the outbreak of the China war in 1937; from then on rural economic life was dictated by the Imperial Rule Assistance Association and leaders on every level were appointed or controlled by the military. The farmer now was forced to become an integral part of a totalitarian national system rigidly controlled from the top down. The entire populace, including the landlords, joined the ranks of the ruled, and up until the end of the war no farmers, even the more influential ones, were able to play a meaningful role in politics.

The Farm as a Conservative Base

The postwar reforms removed farmland from control by the landlord, eliminating his means of manipulating voting behavior among the populace. The farmer was no longer forced to vote for his landlord's candidate merely because he was renting land, yet he still remained very much under the influence of village leaders. Political consciousness did not develop to the point where individuals supported a political party on the strength of their own convictions or voted for candidates without being influenced by others. But even when voters chose to support a candidate recommended by the influential residents of the hamlet, they no longer did so blindly, but voted for candidates who would work for the benefit of the village and the hamlet. This more realistic approach marked the difference between voting behavior in the prewar and postwar periods. Village leaders found it expedient to give full play to a candidate's capacity to work effectively for local interests when supporting those who ran for seats on the prefectural assembly or national Diet. The need to defend candidates' qualifications grew year by year, as hamlet leaders' authority over the votes gradually weakened. Because hamlet control itself gradually weakened, the persuasive powers of a few leaders were no longer sufficient to sway local politics.

On the other hand, the farmer was then and is now myopic in his political judgment. He does not calculate his interests in terms of strata or occupational considerations so much as on the basis of what will benefit his locality as a whole, be it the hamlet or the administrative village. The result of this tendency is that votes inevitably go to the conservative candidate already in power. Before the war the reform parties carried little political weight in the Diet, but they now control more than one-third of the seats. A multi-party system prevailed for ten years until 1955, at which time a coalition of conservatives and a progressive coalition were formed to create left- and right-oriented camps.

Table 47   Political Party Support by Occupational Category (percent)

Occupation	Liberal Democratic		Socialist		Communist		Kōmeitō	
	1976	1972	1976	1972	1976	1972	1976	1972
White-collar and managerial	25	31	19	23	5	4	3	3
Industrial worker	21	23	23	28	5	5	6	5
Shop clerk, etc.	27	31	17	19	4	4	7	6
Self-employed and small proprietor	42	46	8	11	4	3	4	4
Farm, forestry, or fishery	50	52	9	10	1	1	2	1
Unemployed and other	31	36	11	12	3	3	5	6

Source: *Asahi Shimbun*, December 3, 1976, morning edition, " National

The conservative LDP could count on about 60 percent of the vote, and the Japan Socialist party (JSP) about 30 percent. The rural areas were then and remain today the stronghold of LDP support. LDP votes began to decline in the late 1960s, falling to slightly below 50 percent of the total. In the late 1970s, the proliferation of opposition parties has reduced LDP votes to about 40 percent, yet it still retains a majority of seats in the Diet and control of the government.

Despite the decline in rural population, reapportionment of Diet seats has not occurred, with the result that the farm vote now carries disproportionate weight and is still a powerful force. Sustained rural voting strength and the decline of the major opposition party, the JSP, to slightly over 20 percent, have combined to keep the LDP in power. Table 47 shows the results of two surveys made by the *Asahi Shimbun* on support for each political party in the 1972 and 1976 general elections. Clearly, although support has wavered at times, it is safe to say that the majority of farmers vote for the conservative party. Conservatism has become so deeply ingrained that farmers tend to distrust the reform parties, which, as small-property owners, they have difficulty identifying with. The farmer associates the reform parties basically with the interests of unpropertied industrial workers.

Let us now examine the mechanisms that have enabled the

Democratic Socialist		New Liberal Club		Other		Support No Party		No Reply	
1976	1972	1976	1972	1976	1972	1976	1972	1976	1972
5	5	3	—	0	1	24	18	16	15
5	5	2	—	0	0	20	16	18	18
3	3	2	—	0	1	21	16	19	20
4	4	3	—	0	0	19	15	16	17
2	2	1	—	0	0	13	10	22	24
3	4	2	—	0	0	18	14	27	25

Survey on Political Party Support."

LDP to retain its hold on rural areas as the bastion of its political power. As we have seen, the administration of local government which concerns the farmer most is supported by equalization tax rebates and subsidies provided by the prefectural and national governments. No local government body can issue its own bonds without dispensation, so most village and town bonds are backed by national treasury funds. Even a small change in the assessment base for equalization tax rebates has a major effect on local administration, and the size of the subsidy determines how much a village can devote to its economy and industry. If a local government is not authorized to issue bonds, it cannot construct the necessary school and municipal office buildings. To guarantee favorable decisions on these crucial issues, village leaders and mayors must maintain close ties with local representatives in the prefectural assembly and through them with members of the national Diet, who then become the intermediaries in securing funds for their constituency from the prefecture and from government ministries. Clearly those qualified to perform that role most effectively are from the ruling party, the LDP. As long as the reform parties seem unlikely to seize control of the government, rural support will inevitably go to the LDP, but less because it is conservative than because it is the effective holder and manipulator of power.

The village mayor and councilmen, therefore, build city offices and schools and repair roads and bridges using their connections with conservative party Diet members, and the credit goes to the "intermediary," the representative sent by the local constituency to the Diet. As long as local leaders continue to accord him that credit and assure the voters that his efforts for local interests will be sustained, he can depend on voter support. The mayor and councilmen who can personally elicit favors from such representatives can, in turn, be confident of reelection.

For a conservative dietman, acting as intermediary between local interests and the national bureaucracy is one very important method of securing a political base, but there are others as well. Under the present election system, each constituency elects from three to five representatives, and the LDP incumbent must thus compete not only with opposition candidates but with others from his own party. If a dietman cannot rely on the support of the mayor and councilmen only by virtue of his liaison services with the national government, he must play the role of patron. He must extend some form of support when they run for office, which may involve supplying a certain measure of campaign funds. The era of the landlord-controlled farm vote has passed, and individual voters today are much more concerned with their own profit. If a dietman wants to cultivate a secure electoral base, he must supply campaign funds to lower-level village leaders as well.

For this reason, Diet members form supporters' associations made up of leading members of their constituencies which also reach out to form a web of influence among lesser local bosses. When he returns to his constituency, he must hold a gathering of his supporters and entertain them with a banquet. He makes it a practice to send donations to various local associations and for ceremonial events, and if groups of farmers come to Tokyo for sightseeing, he has his staff see that they are properly shown around and entertained. He sends flowers if there is a death in the family of one of his influential supporters, helps their children find jobs, and gives unstinting attention to all types of routine local affairs. Needless to say, the funds he requires to cultivate this kind of constituent support are tremendous.

In return for these forms of support, lesser village leaders together with the mayor and councilmen make certain that the farmers are informed of the achievements of their representatives in the Diet. Ordinarily, such propaganda efforts are accompanied by invitations to drinking parties. At campaign time these district bosses, big and small, can be counted on to work for the dietman's reelection, and the funds involved are usually far in excess of the legal limit.

Where does all this money come from? In large part, it comes from contributions obtained by the party, the leader of the dietman's faction, or the dietman himself from the giant corporations. By this mechanism the LDP extends certain immediate benefits to people at the grass-roots level through the Diet representatives and by taking full advantage of petition politics. Meanwhile, in center stage national politics, the party promotes the interests of big business. The farmers, thus mollified with the crumbs of local benefits and contributions, fail to see that the whole cake is going to big business. In the last several years awareness among farmers that Japanese politics is actually centered on the interests of the large corporations is growing. Nevertheless, they still believe that even the crumbs, however meager, are better than nothing, and stubbornly refuse to abandon them for fear of endangering their future prosperity. They cannot see that the neutral alignment of so-called local interests is not proving beneficial to everyone in the village.

Today's farmer is, however, not satisfied merely with securing local interests. His vision does extend beyond local issues, and if he sees that a problem affecting the entire nation affects him too, he reacts strongly. One such problem is government control of the price of rice. It is an especially vital problem for most of the agricultural cooperatives, for under the present food control system their operations are supported by profits gained from commissions on rice collected for the government's purchase. Through the National Nōkyō Federation, rice-growers exert constant pressure on the government to raise the producer's price of rice. Nōkyō is the farmer's largest political pressure group along with its affiliate, the Farmers' Political Federation (Nōmin Seiji Remmei), and both are indispensable sources of votes for Diet members.

But Nōkyō's pressure group activities are characteristically defensive, partly because it is essentially an economic organization.

Nōkyō seeks to protect the farm economy and to strengthen the base of its own support by continual insistence on increases in the producers' price of rice. Yet it has never demanded policies directed toward achieving stability or development for agriculture. Those elected to village or town Nōkyō positions are considered hamlet representatives, and the cooperative's president is usually an influential local leader who supports the conservative party. Inevitably, officers of the National Nōkyō Federation are conservative also. Its defensive posture vis-à-vis the government prevents Nōkyō from being an effective, constructive pressure group, and it fails to demand reforms in agricultural policy or to direct its efforts toward agricultural development and a stable livelihood for the farmer.

The only organizations that could have served as active pressure groups are the farmers' unions originally set up as political action groups, but as mentioned earlier, these were either disbanded or became dormant after the land reform was carried out. There is a national center of farmers' unions which supports the reformist parties, but its grass-roots organizations in the villages and towns are at present inactive. A lack of organizational dynamism in the left-wing parties is partly to blame, but the farmers themselves have too many vested interests in the continuation of the conservative status quo to develop a serious commitment to building a farmer union-type of organization.

Thus, national politics have never given first priority to the welfare of the farmer. Because rural areas are an important source of votes, the LDP presents itself as being oriented toward agriculture. LDP representatives are quick to assert their party's concern for rural modernization and farmer welfare, but such claims are made to combat the tendency among the younger generations, which are less bound by family authority and vote more independently, to move toward the reform parties. It is this LDP farm policy that has produced Japan's huge rice surplus. The government is forced to maintain policies guaranteed to antagonize farmers: curtailing acreage planted to rice and trying to hold down annual price increases. While the rural areas were once the unwavering base of conservative party support, it is now quite possible that a major shift will occur in its voting preferences. Such change will not be rapid, for the mechanisms of conservative power will not easily be dismantled, but the farming population is heading into a dead end, and the knowledge of that fate is strengthening both the farmers' distrust of the conservative party and their political acumen. It is now reasonable to expect that farmers will begin to take steps to move the government toward new directions more favorable to their interests.

Postwar National Government

Soon after the war, efforts were concentrated on raising production to alleviate food shortages which persisted for a long time, and this policy continued steadily for several years. But when the situation improved, emphasis on production was abandoned. From about 1953 on, farm policy began to lose its sense of direction. When the economy shifted from recovery to growth, farm policy had to move too, away from stress on higher production of the staple grains. In 1956, the government adopted a Comprehensive Program for the Development of New Farm, Mountain, and Fishing Villages, but the program did little more than call for "the right crop in the right region" and what could have been the turning point for agriculture ended up stymied.

The abrupt turning point eventually came as the gap between agriculture and industry widened with the sudden leaps of economic growth. On the basis of findings of a 1959 government Commission on Basic Problems of Agriculture, Forestry, and Fishing, the Basic Law of Agriculture was passed in 1961. The preamble to the Basic Law states: "It is a duty arising from our concern for the public welfare, and an indispensable adjunct to the mission of agriculture and of farmers in our country, to ensure that the disadvantages resulting from the natural economic and social limitations of agriculture are eliminated, to promote the modernization and rationalization of agriculture while respecting the free will and initiative of those engaged in it, and make it possible for the nation's farmers to enjoy a healthy and cultured livelihood commensurate with that of other members of the population." The purpose of the law was to "define a new direction for agriculture and to clarify the objectives of agricultural policy."

Based on the provisions of this law, the government under-took the so-called Structural Reform of Agriculture Program. It was aimed at tackling the problems caused by the fragmentation of farmlands which had effectively stymied agricultural production. Japanese agriculture had grown incapable of competing on the international market and had become an obstacle to economic development. If the reform of agriculture could be achieved cheaply, it would be in the interests of both agriculture and of big business as well. The program was designed to adjust the base of the agricultural production system and introduce modern management facilities by providing subsidies from the government. In the case of wet rice production, to give a simplified example, fields would be consolidated into blocks averaging 30 ares, and paddy cultivation would be mechanized using tractors. By these measures, the program sought to bring agricultural incomes up to a par with those of other industries.

However, the Basic Law upon which the government's program of agricultural reform was based was not comprehensive enough to pave the way for a real transformation of Japanese agriculture. The basic premise of the investigatory commission was the principle of equalization of incomes, and it presumed the continuing out-migration of farmers into other industries. It sought to foster independent agricultural enterprise, and concomitantly envisioned the growth of cooperative farming operations. Even then, farm income was to be brought closer to the industrial level not by policies that increased agricultural income per se, but through the easier method of raising farm household income. For that reason, the program did not include concrete measures to help the part-time farmer move completely out of agriculture. It also set no clear directions for agricultural development, and as facts would later show, the number of independent farm operators did not increase. In implementing the program, the standardization of government guidance tended to discourage independent initiatives by farmers. Modernization of agriculture through mechanization would actually be made possible by the large-scale movement of families out of agriculture but the program failed on that point. It never achieved structural reform and could not overcome the essential weaknesses and inconsistencies of Japanese agriculture. Moreover, almost a decade after the program's inception, the 1970 settlement survey showed that it had been implemented in only 11 percent of settlements throughout the nation. In area, the 1975 census showed that after ten years, the structural improvement program had affected only 11 percent of all wet rice paddies and only 7 percent of dry fields.

Although the structural reform program was frequently criticized as victimizing the poor farmer, it cannot be so simplistically described. Japanese agriculture cannot make a breakthrough no matter how hard small, part-time farmers try to work cooperatively. A structural reform program should not be aimed at wiping out the small, part-time farmer, but at making it possible for him to find secure employment and adequate income in some other occupation so that he could feel free to cut ties with agriculture completely. In addition, a parallel program to organize remaining farmers into a cooperative system must be worked out to make structural reform of agriculture possible. The program failed partly because it was carried out in only a few villages. Further, no assistance was given farmers to find secure, full-time jobs elsewhere, and most preferred to take part-time work away from the farm rather than risk giving up agriculture altogether. Still, these problems should not be attributed to the reform program itself.

The regional development policy discussed earlier is also related to the failure of the reform. It encouraged cities and towns to bring industry into their areas, but it did nothing to develop agriculture. It would have been a positive contribution if factories set up locally had absorbed farmers into their full-time labor force and allowed the people remaining in agriculture to consolidate their lands and modernize production. But even when factories moved in, they did not employ as large a number of local people as had been expected. The more modern the factory, the fewer job opportunities it provided, and in most cases, farmers could be employed only when there were openings for unskilled workers. The number of jobs in trucking and hauling for the new factories that were built grew, but such jobs were hardly well paying and could not provide a secure livelihood. Therefore, the most significant effect of the incoming factories was a rise in the number of part-time farmers.

While many farmers left agriculture, those remaining who wanted to expand their acreage could not do so because industrialization had inflated land values beyond the reach of most of the farmers. Moreover, it was they, as well as the local resident, who had to bear the cost of preparing factory sites, thus further hampering investment in agriculture. Many naively believed that future revenues from corporate taxes would one day finance local improvements for agriculture. Planners did not fully consider the urbanizing effects of industrialization and the added demands it would make on local resources. The benefits of regional development through industrialization, at least given the current nature of industry, cannot be channeled into agricultural development, but even so factories did not move into rural areas in large numbers.

Neither agricultural nor regional development policy has brought brighter prospects for the Japanese village. The Basic Law of Agriculture reached a stalemate less than a decade after it was promulgated. A coherent farm policy could not be achieved while annual hikes in the price of rice persisted and huge rice surpluses forced cutbacks in production. Rice cultivation has reached a definite impasse, but to convert fields to other crops and shift production is very difficult. Dairy farming has been expanded virtually to its limit and dairy products are actually in oversupply, and fruit-growers are faced with increasing competition from imports as a result of trade liberalization. The problems of agriculture have reached an extremely serious crisis, but while there is much talk of a "comprehensive farm policy," the policy objectives have yet to be defined.

The "comprehensive farm policy" is designed to: 1) ensure stable supply in response to trends in food needs for products in all categories; 2) effectively combine appropriate pricing mechanisms, structural adjustments, and production methods to achieve a balance between supply and demand; and 3) provide systematic and integrated guidelines for processing, distribution, and consumption, as well as production. This policy shows little sign of success, however, and to complement it the government has undertaken measures to encourage rural industrialization. These measures were aimed at increasing the opportunities for stable employment of people in local areas and promoting agriculture together with establishment of new factories. But as the rate of economic growth continues to decelerate, the original plans grow harder to fulfill. Most likely the implementation of those plans will produce no more than a large-scale version of local industrial development projects, in which small industries move into rural areas and pay minimum wages to farm housewives for part-time work, exploiting the farmer's need for cash income but doing little to resolve his basic plight.

Only massive capital investment can save Japanese agriculture from declining further toward the crisis that looms ahead. If farming is to be conducted in an economically rational manner without the need for special aids, it is crucial that the agricultural base be given a firm footing. Agriculture served very well as the foundation upon which Japan's economy developed, but without truly drastic measures it will not be possible to restore its solid base. The government pursues only short-term goals and continues to support the interests of big business, so that such measures seem utterly impossible. Rural society underwent tremendous change during the period of high growth, but the national government formulated no effective policies to deal with those changes.

Political Attitudes of the Farmer

Social Characteristics

The traditional social characteristics of the Japanese farmer were the product of the *ie* based on the unilineal, patriarchal family system, and the community-like hamlet dominated by status stratification. As described earlier, one of the functions of the *ie* system was to preserve order and harmony under the authoritarian control of the househead. Members were assigned places according to seniority by age and sex. But that harmony was not one of freedom and ease, but of frustration and constraint. Likewise, on the village level, rigid distinctions of class and status defined the traditional social order. Under this order individual desires were suppressed and the family kept its "place" in observance of the social rules which upheld the hierarchical system. Peace in the village meant obedience to the ruling class. The harmony of the village, like that of the family, was not a pleasant, happy one, but held the villagers to a rigid code of social behavior.

Thus the farmer's personality was molded by resignation to assigned social status necessary to support the welfare of the group. This aversion to anything that would upset family or community harmony inevitably promotes the tendency for conformism. In the customary pattern of behavior, the most expedient course of action was that which followed the majority. Farmer's actions revolved around the social norms of the hamlet, and this conformity to custom formed the farmer's traditionalistic and conservative character. Status consciousness created the habit of deference to authority. In the hierarchical social order passed down through the generations, submission to authority produced feelings of inferiority which were compensated for by an attitude of superiority toward those of lower strata. An important aspect of the Japanese farmer's social personality was his care not to step beyond the confines of his social status.

This pattern began to change with the growth of capitalism. As the money economy permeated the rural districts, the farmer began to calculate his interests in monetary terms. As closer contacts developed between the closed, self-sufficient rural village and urban society, farmers' expectations for a better life began to rise. The capitalist economy broke down the ridigity of the social hierarchy in the village and transformed the pattern of family status. In this process of change, in order to satisfy their growing expectations, farmers sought to expand the framework of the *ie* through greater efforts to raise the socioeconomic status of the family within the hierarchical social system.

A sense of self-interest was born, though it remained dormant as long as the communal order of the *mura* society controlled the behavior of its members. As farm productivity increased, the communal mode of production became less common and farmers could conduct farm management more independently. The community retained control over forests and irrigation, however, and the farmer could not be completely independent of other members of the hamlet. The struggle to raise family status was not carried on openly, however, and instead of fostering healthy individualism, it gave rise to a somewhat distorted egoism. Even through such self-interested efforts, however, it was very difficult to succeed in raising one's family status. The size of inherited family land imposed a limit on what such effort could achieve, and many had to resign themselves to those limitations. Liberation from authoritarianism and from conformity to the social norms that governed rural life did not come until the land reform.

The changes in rural society brought about by the postwar land reform had enormous impact on the social personality of the farmer. The egoism of the farmer was further encouraged by the collapse of the social hierarchy brought about by the reform and brought to the surface as the communal character of the hamlet broke down. As the solidarity of the hamlet weakened, conformity became less important, and it was much easier to act in ways that ran counter to custom. The collapse of the landlord system removed the social imperative of unquestioning acceptance of the landlord's authority, for he no longer controlled the land.

After the war it became difficult to restrain the farmer's impulses to seek a better livelihood, impulses which had been thwarted by his status in the social hierarchy and which now blossomed and diversified. Aspirations were inflated all the more as urbanization progressed, and farm families sought to satisfy awakened desires by augmenting their cash income. Farmers whose holdings were too small to permit any rise in income tended to take part-time jobs outside of agriculture. Increased differentiation of the farming population contributed to the weakening of hamlet solidarity, and different rural groups began to assert their own interests, making it difficult to maintain hamlet holism. The traditional order faced inevitable change, and this is another factor in the weakening of rural conformism.

Yet the burgeoning spirit of self-interest did not develop into rational individualism. The system of the *ie*, while breaking down, continued to exert some influence, and the hamlet, while it lost its cohesiveness, did not entirely disintegrate. Self-interest never transcended family interest, and *buraku* egoism would not allow the abandonment of hamlet solidarity. The reason for this is that the farm household economy never allowed the farmers to develop individuality, and that agricultural production never rose sufficiently to enable the family to become independent of the hamlet. Moreover, although conditions had changed somewhat, the conformist character of the farmer which had been molded over the centuries could not be eradicated overnight. Neither individualism of rational action based on an independent standard of behavior nor democracy premised on rational cooperation and mutual respect of individual autonomy had yet affected the character of the Japanese farmer.

Farm society grew more heterogeneous, but its various functional groups continued to exist without becoming distinct from the hamlet. The principle of hamlet holism in group organization ceased to be meaningful, yet was still artifically preserved. Nōkyō enlists every farm family in its membership, from fulltime professional farmers to those whose main income comes from non-farming sources, and includes even non-farmers as associate members. Because it tries to serve the varied needs of so many different groups, Nōkyō cannot give highest priority to agriculture, and its activities are often ineffectual as a result. Had the farmers developed a truly democratic consciousness, they could have made Nōkyō into their own organization aimed specifically at answering the needs of agriculture; instead it provides a plethora of services but offers no basic solutions to problems.

On the issue of cooperative projects, certain to become a major problem for Japanese agriculture, there is still a strong tendency for cooperative cultivation groups to organize on the basis of the hamlet, insofar as conditions permit. Even in cases where their membership cannot be identical with hamlet membership, it is very difficult to envision the formation of new democratically based groups. As I have described above, cooperation in traditional Japan was only made possible by the suppression of individual interests and the assertion of authoritarian control. This traditional sense of cooperation, however, is still very much alive. But cooperation today will not succeed unless it is democratic and fair, and sustained by independent individuals who respect the interests of others. Yet the Japanese farmer has not developed this sense of himself and others in society. From now on, particularly as lands are handed on to the younger generation, part-time farmers will lease their lands to full-time farmers and the scale of farms will grow, but agricultural development will not be achieved without the continued use of some kinds of cooperative projects. Cultivation can now be done with large tractors and agricultural tasks can be commissioned to specialists. It is already becoming clear that in this course of events farmers still have not developed a rational approach to their profession.

Amid the profound changes that have occurred in agriculture since 1945, farmers still retain a deeply ingrained social and traditional character. The farmer continues to be content if the interests of his locality are satisfied and if the price of rice rises regularly. There is still no movement on the part of farmers to protest the monopoly of the benefits of economic growth by big business.

The Political Consciousness of the Farmer

It is often said that a farmer has two souls: one is that of the manual laborer and the other that of the petit bourgeois who owns land and equipment and manages his farm independently. If the farmer stopped to consider how poor the return he receives is in proportion to his own input, he might develop the anti-establishment, revolutionary spirit that develops among the exploited classes. But as long as his awareness remains dormant and he remains passive to the status quo, his petit-bourgeois mentality will dominate, preserving conservatism in rural Japan.

Bound by the constraints of the *ie* system and by the communal life of the hamlet, the conservatism of the Japanese farmer has a long tradition. For the farmer, land was not merely a means of production but the property of the household, the legacy of generations. He believed it was his destiny to cultivate the land of his forefathers with care and to carry on the family tradition of farming. As long as he could continue this life style, he would not resist government power. Like the powers of nature, the authority of rulers was not something to be resisted; he never questioned that it was his lot to be among the governed.

One would have expected this pattern of farmer consciousness to undergo profound change with the development of the capitalist economy following the Meiji Restoration, but that change was frustrated by the ideology of *nōhonshugi*, or agrarian fundamentalism. This ideology was essentially anti-agrarian in nature, but it provided relief and psychological comfort for farmers who had developed an inferiority complex in a capitalist society. The landlord ideology of agrarian fundamentalism sang the praises of the long-suffering, hard-working farmer content with a low standard of living, effectively putting blinders on the farmer's political consciousness. The prewar political consciousness of the farmer has been sustained almost as blindly, save for the brief spark of the farmers' union movement, up to the present.

Japan's defeat in 1945 rendered the ideology of agrarian fundamentalism impotent. The rationale which justified the poor compensation received from farming in comparison with other professions because it was a "noble calling" could no longer be supported. It took some time for the farmers themselves to overcome the deeply ingrained patterns of *nōhonshugi*, but Table 48 shows how radically opinions have since changed. Uncompensated family labor has come under severe attack, and farming is now thought of as an enterprise that should show a profit. At long last the old-fashioned belief of the farmer that consumption is a vice and thrift a virtue and that in spite of poverty one must continually redouble one's efforts is finally being discarded. Farmers have tried to raise productivity and create better lives, but their efforts could not close the gap between agriculture and the other industrial sectors, and rapid economic growth opened the gap even wider.

Table 48   Views on Agrarian Fundamentalism (percent)

| | Akita | | Okayama | |
	1953	1968	1953	1968
Agriculture is foundation of nation	78.2	53.7	65.9	35.4
Agriculture is not foundation of nation	13.1	23.6	25.6	42.0
Can't say either way	4.9	13.4	5.9	18.1
Don't know	3.8	9.3	2.6	4.5

Farmers have become convinced that government policy is biased entirely in favor of industry, leaving agriculture to fend for itself. An examination of a series of surveys made by my colleagues in 1962 and 1963, when the national growth rate was being accelerated by the government's income-doubling policy, shows that almost half the farmers believed that the main focus of the policy was big business (Table 49). They were well aware of the government's preoccupation with industrial growth, as reflected in ineffectual farm policy, and realized that the economic gap between agriculture and other industries would not diminish. According to surveys made when the structural improvement program was moving into high gear throughout the nation, less than 10 percent of the rural population believed the government was sincerely working on behalf of agriculture. Today, farmers clearly distrust the national government.

Table 49 Farmers' Views on National Government, 1962–63

Policy of Economic Growth	Percentage
I support it	17.9
It mainly benefits big business	48.5
It has been a failure since it started	17.6
Other	1.5
Don't know	14.5
National Farm Policy	
Will narrow gap between agriculture and other sectors	12.6
Will widen the gap	47.4
Will effect no change	10.4
Don't know	17.7

Why, then, is rural Japan still a stronghold of LDP support? It is not, as is sometimes argued, because rural political attitudes are still dominated by a traditional pattern of apathy. Such apathy may have prevailed in the fifteen-odd years after the war, but understandably so, since the consciousness of passive subjects is not easily altered. Particularly concerning issues which immediately concerned them, the farmer could hardly have been called apathetic. Their attitude was quite the opposite of the urban intelligentsia who, while interested in the problems of the whole nation or of the international community, tend to pay little attention to issues that directly affect them. Notably, the farmers have recently begun to take very clear stands on national policy, and there has been a significant decline in the percentage of rural respondents who answer "Don't know" in opinion surveys. They are now clearly aware that conservative party politics is fundamentally unconcerned with agriculture and designed primarily for the benefit of big business. Yet they continue to support the conservative party. Voting patterns as well as surveys concerning party affiliation consistently show that support of the conservative party is widespread among farmers.

The reasons for continuing LDP support by the farm bloc must be sought in the mechanisms described above. The petit-bourgeois mentality of the farmer makes him shun the reform parties with which the industrial workers identify and his concern with the mundane and immediate interests of his locality lures him to support of the party in power. His choice is also influenced by a resigned acceptance of the fact that agriculture becomes an increasingly less important sector in the process of economic growth and that government policy is bound to focus on the interests of big business.

Furthermore, the farmer's standard of living has actually risen, despite the tremendous changes in and overall decline of agriculture. He attributes this to the LDP. While the gap between industry and agriculture has widened, per household farm income reached rough parity with wage-earning laborers in small cities by the latter 1960s. By the early 1970s it was equal with the national average for urban laborers. Rising expectations have not made the farmer's livelihood much easier, but the increase in household income has helped farmers to fulfill their aspirations and raise consumption at much faster rates than the urban worker. In a national survey on attitudes conducted in 1965 by the Ministry of Agriculture and Forestry, close to half the respondents stated that farming could be profitable if managed properly. This is lower than the 1963 figures but still well over 40 percent. During that two-year period the number of farmers who stated preference for full-time farming declined from 58 to 44 percent, but as long as the farm family can maintain its standard of living through part-time farming, political attitudes or behavior are not likely to change significantly. Since those surveys were made, however, farmers have suffered several major setbacks resulting from government policy. These include, for example, the failure of the government to raise the price of rice in 1969 and the paddy reduction program in 1970. The impact of such measures cannot be calculated fully yet, but they may effect change in rural political behavior and attitudes.

Change in Political Attitudes

In the 1965 attitudinal survey by the agriculture and forestry ministry, 77 percent of the respondents expressed the opinion that agriculture is less profitable than any other industry, and about 40 percent of these stated that there was no hope of improving conditions no matter how hard they worked. Six percent of the total thought agriculture was more profitable than any other industry, and 10 percent said they saw no difference. Younger respondents, particularly those with relatively large farms, tended to believe that conditions would improve. If farmers with large-scale operations dominate rural political trends, the conservative hold will remain strong. The slowdown in the rate of increase of the rice price and production cutbacks have not affected attitudes among younger farmers very much. In the 1975 agriculture and forestry ministry survey focusing on the heirs to independent, full-time farm households and households intending to establish independent operations, more than 80 percent said they preferred farming as a way of life and would continue it permanently (see Table 50).

Survey results seem to indicate that the full-time farmer is not ready to drop his support for the LDP, which he believes has, on the whole, helped him. The 1965 survey indicated that more than 70 percent of farmers operating 1.5 hectares or more were confident of their future in farming. Their optimism was shared by 49 percent of those who obtained most of their income from farming, by 33 percent of those who obtained most income from non-farm sources, and from 64 percent of full-time farmers. This same sentiment is reflected in the survey made in 1975. More than any other group, perhaps, wealthier full-time farmers have benefited from and feel secure under the conservative government. It is easier for this group to borrow funds and receive assistance on interest payments from local government. They also benefit more than any other group of farmers from lobbying ac-

Table 50 Farming Heirs' Views on the Future of Agriculture, 1975

Farming as an Occupation	Percentage
I feel real purpose in life in farming	83.2
I am not really interested in farming, but it is the family business, so I will continue	8.3
I am not interested in farming, and I want to leave it	0.9
Will continue farming while working on a side job	7.4
Other	0.2
Reasons for feeling purpose in life in farming	
Can operate the way I wish	65.1
It is the best occupation to test my abilities	17.2
Like working outdoors with plants and animals	12.8
Food production contributes to society	1.9
Farming is a profitable business	1.4
Other	1.6

tivities for promotion of local interests. These wealthy full-time farmers have even acquired a self-image, or an illusion, of being active participants in the political process by virtue of their close connections with people of power.

Among part-time farmers whose income is largely from other, relatively stable jobs, some have been influenced by their labor unions and support reform parties. Among small part-time operators, support for reform parties is relatively high. But because they supply part of their own food and own homes, their standard of living is on a par with large-scale operators. True political reformism is not likely to become a strong force among these landowning workers.

It is also revealing that even the hard-pressed, overworked part-time farmers, who earn most income outside, have not shown particular interest in the progressive parties. Their income is unstable, and they have no time left for involvement in politics. This is the group with the most conservative political attitudes, and in which the traditional pattern of political apathy is still prevalent. Without any clear-cut political views of their own, they tend to follow the lead of large-scale, full-time farmers and vote for the conservatives. On the other hand, the part-time farmer who supports the reform parties has neither the power nor the intent to draw the others into the political ranks of organized labor. They do not have the spare time to organize opposition to conservative party supporters who hold some hamlet positions and work in the hamlet all day. Their relatively secure economic position removes one source of motivation to campaign in the village for support to reform parties. In the end their political activity is limited to voting for candidates supported by their labor organization, in this way acting against the wishes of the village bosses.

In the last fifteen years, political attitudes have remained virtually unchanged, and conservative votes remain at about the same level. Rural support for the reform parties has increased slightly, but in 1969, just before the government announced new measures to deal with overproduction of rice, farmers strongly backed the LDP in hopes of some kind of compensation from government. The conservatives won an overwhelming victory in the ensuing December general election. As the period of high economic growth advanced, the opposition parties expected change in rural LDP support, but they were disappointed. The reform parties were not pragmatic enough in their approach to immediate problems; they placed too much emphasis on abstract left-wing theory and heavy support from labor union and urban interests. Partly because of renewed LDP efforts to regain support lost in the countryside, and partly because attitudes and behavior tend to change less rapidly than social or economic conditions, there was not a marked swing toward the reformist positions. Again, many farmers find it difficult to break away from their support for the conservatives, because they are entangled in a web of personal relations characteristic of rural society. And to translate any change in attitudes into behavior also takes time. In any case, the attitudes and behavior of farmers are probably going to remain constant in the absence of a major threat to their way of life. If, for example, the middle-strata farmers degenerate in large numbers into landless workers, while upper-strata, full-time farmers have their hopes shattered of expanding their independent operations, then overall attitudes may change.

The crisis of Japanese farming, which has surfaced most recently in the form of rice overproduction, has influenced attitudes, but not in a revolutionary way. Upper-strata farmers still cling to their illusion of operating a large-scale and profitable farm enterprise. Although the differentiation of middle-strata farmers is increasing the number of landowning laborers, in probably only a few instances will the trend develop to the extent that these men abandon farming and become purely laborers. The reform parties themselves are doing little on behalf of the farmer. Their overly dogmatic approach to agriculture appeals to the farmer little. Although the progressives have attacked the structural reform program as a device to eliminate the poor farmers and have advocated increases in the rice price just as the conservative farm-based politicans do, they have developed no program that will attract the farmer.

The conservative party won a major victory in the 1969 general election but lost a large number of seats two years later in the House of Councilors election. In the 1976 general election, the opposition made further gains and by 1977, in the House of Councilors election, the LDP just barely held onto its majority. Clearly the conservative hold on politics is weakening, not the least because the agricultural prefectures are no longer dependable bases of LDP support. This in turn indicates a change in the political attitudes of the farmer, but the great bulk of the farm vote by no means has shifted to the opposition. The intense dissatisfaction with government agricultural policy comes out only in a slightly more critical stand vis-à-vis the LDP. Depending on what the LDP does from now on, the party might check the erosion of its rural stronghold. If, on the other hand, the reform parties are to encourage the shift, they must revise their farm policy, make active efforts to build a political machine in the rural areas, and constantly cultivate support in the farm village to increase their votes. Although the conservatives' politics of personal connections and favors does show signs of weakening in the rural areas, it is still deeply entrenched. The reformists must work many times harder to uproot and replace a rural establishment that has been in place for a very long time.

The leftist parties are also handicapped by an inadequate appreciation of the critical situation of Japanese agriculture. Today's conditions cannot be ameliorated merely by encouraging more cooperative work methods among farmers and doing nothing to radically change the present status quo. Small farm operations are no longer viable. The future will become brighter only when the many, many small farmers still hanging on leave agriculture completely and those who remain join in organized, cooperative endeavors. The farmer who can be called a farmer in the genuine sense of the word is aware of the difficulties ahead and knows that agriculture carried out on an individual basis is not feasible. Once the system of human relations that traditionally governed politics in the rural village is recognized openly as having served its purpose in another era and another economy, the farmers' awareness of present and future realities can be transformed into concrete action. I think we will then see a dramatic change in rural political attitudes and voting behavior. Yet before that day comes, Japanese agriculture must surmount many more difficulties and crises.

Index

administrative office, postwar, 172
administrative village, 71, 77
affinal relations, 68, 69–70
aging problem, 13
agrarian fundamentalism, 17–18. *See also nōhonshugi*
agricultural association, 155
Agricultural Extension Service, 8
Agricultural Land Adjustment Law, 7
agricultural practice union, 41, 81–82, 88–89, 103, 107, 109, 117, 126, 127–28, 141–42
agricultural prices, 5. *See also* rice, price of
agricultural production, 200
agriculture: declining priority of, 185; as family enterprise, 4; funds for, 179, 180; future of, 14, 208–9; influence of industrialization on, 3; lack of program to develop, 195; postwar reform in, 193–94
allowances, for hamlet officials, 117, 141
amae, 37
amalgamation: attempts at, of hamlet assets, 152; and decline in council members, 169; disputes concerning, 165–66; financial deficit following, 178; Meiji, 145, 164; postwar, 161; reasons for, 146, 164–65; statistics on, 147, 164, 166
anti-landlord movement, 140, 162
anti-pollution measures, 176, 180

Basic Law of Agriculture, 193, 194–95, 196
"bed town," 175
blue-collar: income, 18; worker, 15

bonds, 189
boundaries, 77–78
branch family, 28; and *dōzoku*, 59; establishment of, 60; in Meiji era, 67–68. *See also* servant branch family
bride: assumes *ie* duties, 36–37; as producer of heir, 34–35; qualifications of, 34; relationship with husband, 36, 37; status of, 35–36; visits home by, 36
bunke, 30, 31. *See also* branch family
buraku, 71, 153, 167; as administrative unit, 78–79, 110
by-laws, of village, 110, 115–16

campaigning: funds for, 190; methods of, 177–78
capitalist economy, 17, 65, 74, 130, 139, 150, 151, 160, 184, 185, 198, 202
car ownership, 19
chamber of commerce, 170
child raising, 37
chōnaikai, 151
citizen, definition of, 147
citizens' movement, 176, 180
Civil Code: inheritance provisions in, 31, 44–45, 50; and marriage, 35; postwar revisions in, 38–39
civil servants, 172
class conflict, 158
commerce and industry, expenditures on, 170
Commission on Basic Problems of Agriculture, Forestry, and Fishing, 193
commodity economy, 85, 121
commodity market, 74, 83